ZOOM

PERSONAL IMAGES AND INSIGHTS

FROM THE STARS OF FORMULA 1®

MW01703131

CREDITS

© Zoom Event Management Limited, 2015

Editors: Caroline Reid, Christian Sylt
Design: Stewart Wheeler
Editorial assistants: Kate Hewitt, Katy Fairman

Personality portraits and cover: Sutton Motorsport Images
Sutton Motorsport Images is the world's largest independent motorsport picture agency. Its archive of over 4m transparencies, with a searchable on-line digital archive of over 900,000 images, spans the entire history of motorsport. **www.sutton-images.com**

Printed by: Thomas Graphics, Inc., 9501 North I.H.-35, Austin, Texas 78753.
www.thomasgraphicsinc.com

All rights reserved. No part of this publication may be reproduced, stored in a retrieval system or transmitted in any form or by any means, electronic, mechanical, photocopying, recording or otherwise, without the prior permission of the publishers. This publication is sold subject to the condition that it shall not, by way of trade or otherwise, be lent, re-sold, hired out, or otherwise, without the publisher's prior consent in any form of binding or cover other than that in which it is published and without a similar condition including this condition being imposed on the subsequent purchaser.

F1, FORMULA 1, FIA FORMULA ONE WORLD CHAMPIONSHIP, GRAND PRIX and related marks are trade marks of Formula One Licensing BV, a Formula One group company. All rights reserved. Used with kind permission of Formula One Licensing BV.

Published by Money Sport Media Limited on behalf of Zoom Event Management Limited
ISBN: 978-0-9932229-0-0

CONTENTS

FOREWORD

FROM BERNIE ECCLESTONE

The superstars of Formula One are the biggest names in racing. They are renowned for their daring manoeuvres on track and their jet-set lifestyles away from it but few people ever find out what really makes them tick. What hobbies do they have? Where do they go on holiday? Do they have any pets? These are questions that anyone can relate to and this book gives the answers.

All of the team principals and drivers who compete in F1 were asked to take a photograph of whatever they wanted and the results are shown on the following pages. They provide windows onto the world beyond the track and are views that no one else could get.

You can admire the same sunset that Red Bull Racing team principal Christian Horner saw over the sea outside his holiday home in southern England. Last year's champion Lewis Hamilton takes us on a tour of the rugged jogging trails in Colorado where he trains during his down time. My photos give you a look in and around my house in Switzerland.

It has all been done for a wonderful cause because the sale of this book benefits Great Ormond Street Hospital Children's Charity and all the photos have been signed and sold at an auction in aid of it.

The F1 Group and Ecclestone family have been supporting Great Ormond Street Hospital for many years and we are proud to be able to help with the tremendous work they do. Every year the hospital treats nearly 300,000 sick children and by buying this book you are helping them keep it up. You are also getting a glimpse into a side of F1 that isn't shown on television and as you will see, it isn't all about fast cars and champagne.

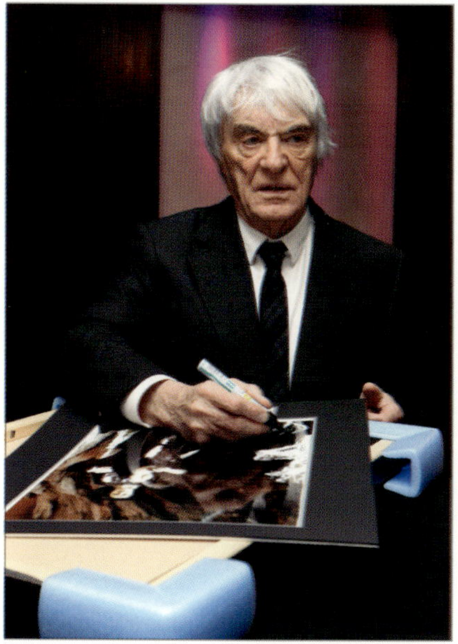

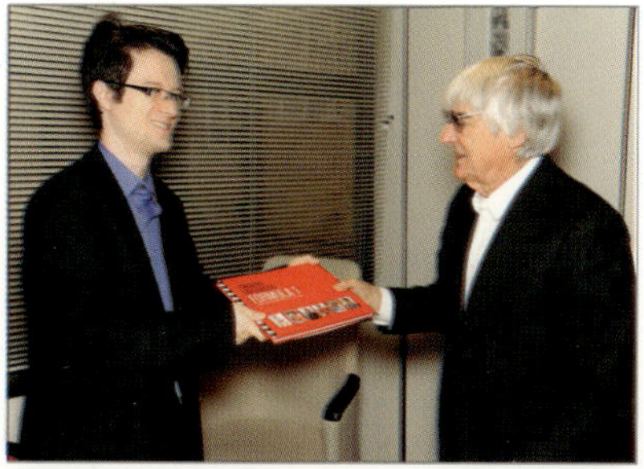

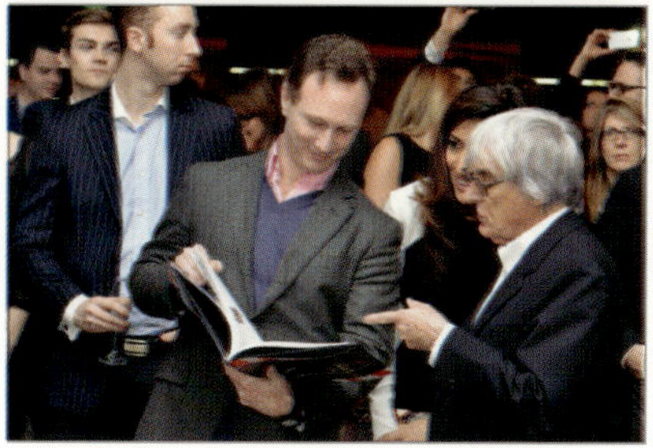

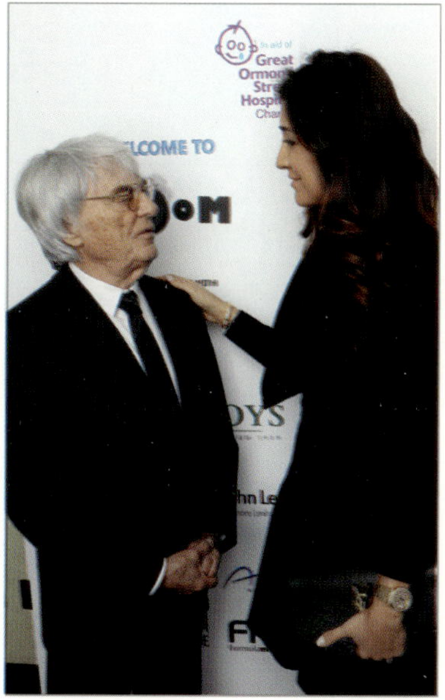
In aid of
Great

INTRODUCTION

Zoom: Where F1® And Charity Clicks

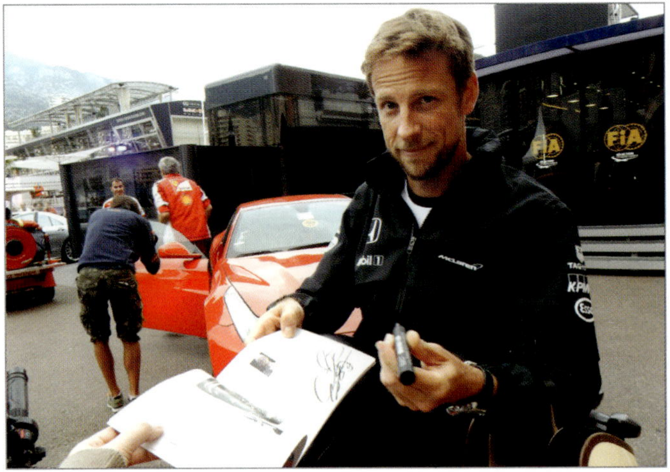

Zoom has entered its third year in 2015 and the success of the initiative is down to a very simple idea.

The concept was created in late 2012 by Christian Sylt and Caroline Reid, authors of Formula One's industry monitor Formula Money. They realised that although there are many charity auctions in sport they all tend to follow a similar pattern.

The items on offer are usually signed photos of the athletes or signed kit that they use. They often raise a great deal of money but usually tell the buyer little about the sports star who signed them. Zoom was created to rectify that by turning the tables and asking all the drivers and team principals in F1 to take photographs which would then be signed and put up for auction.

Zoom is the first and only auction of signed photos taken by the stars of any sport. It is also one of very few events, except for a Grand Prix, which involves all of the teams and all of the drivers. They join forces in order to benefit a very worthwhile cause: raising money for charity. All the proceeds from the Zoom auction go towards life-saving and pioneering projects.

Supporting charity has long been a key part of F1 and is close to the heart of the sport's chief executive Bernie Ecclestone. One of the most important steps in establishing Zoom was getting Bernie's support and the participation of all the drivers and team principals followed suit.

Christian has known Bernie for more than a decade and his support of Zoom has been invaluable. Such has been the level of interest in it that former F1 drivers and champions, as well as commentators and designers, have also participated.

All the photographers put their heart into the challenge, resulting in a diverse collection of photos which show both insider views from the track and personal memories from outside the world of racing.

The photos take you on a journey through the lives of F1's superstars. They give a window onto the serene jogging trails around Lewis Hamilton's favourite holiday resort in Aspen and allow you to watch as Nico Rosberg's helmet is painted. You can even sample the vista that Bernie sees of his garden from the window of his Swiss chalet whilst Jenson Button's snap of his race seat is a view that only a select few will ever see in person.

Since it was established Zoom is proud to have raised more than £50,000 for charity and all of the F1 teams, team bosses and drivers play an essential part in making this happen. We sincerely thank them along with everyone else who has donated a photo to the project.

It has all been done for a wonderful reason because the sale of this book benefits charity and all the photos have been signed and sold at auction in aid of a good cause.

The F1 Group and Ecclestone family have been supporting Great Ormond Street Hospital for many years and we are proud to be able to help with the tremendous work they do. Every year the hospital treats nearly 300,000 sick children and by buying this book you are helping them keep it up. You are also getting a glimpse into a side of F1 that isn't shown on television and as you will see, it isn't all about fast cars and champagne.

A MESSAGE FROM AUSTIN

Welcome to the 2015 United States Grand Prix! I am delighted to have the opportunity to introduce this special edition of the Zoom book and share a few words on a project that is close to COTA's heart.

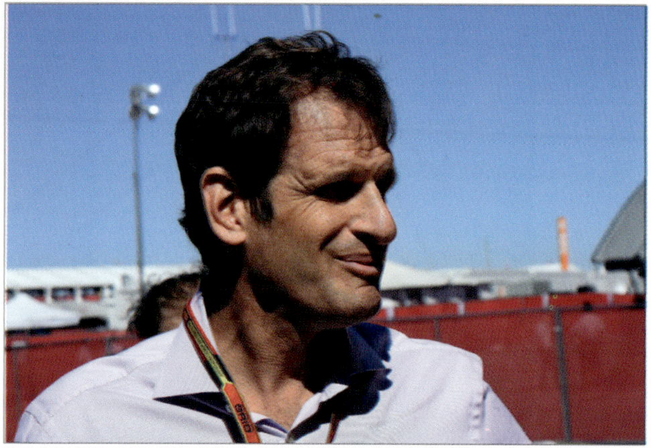

Circuit of the Americas became the Official Grand Prix Partner of Zoom last year and is proud to support this initiative that mixes the glamour of Formula One with the art of photography all in aid of a good cause. Through partnering the Zoom initiative, we are delighted to put COTA at the centre of a project that unites the biggest names in the sport.

The concept of Zoom is unique. All F1's drivers and team principals were each asked to take a snapshot of their world and each one gives a unique insight into the personal side of F1. We all take photos so anyone can relate to these images and that reflects our mission at COTA as it brings F1 a step closer to the fans.

In this book you will find many different images showing the drivers at work and at play, alone and in crowds, at home and in all the corners of the world. COTA itself has also featured in the images, including the photograph on the right which was taken by the host of Zoom, the UK's F1 presenter Suzi Perry.

Suzi took the photo at the race in 2013 and it shows her and her crew enjoying themselves at the track shortly after encountering Friends star Matt LeBlanc, who is seen pictured on the cameraman's cell phone. It captures what COTA is about: fun, glamour and, in Suzi's words, "a fabulous event, live music everywhere and terrific weather."

As we enter our fourth race, none of that has changed. I hope that you enjoy looking at these images as much as I did and thank you for attending our race.

Bobby Epstein,
Chairman,
Circuit of the Americas

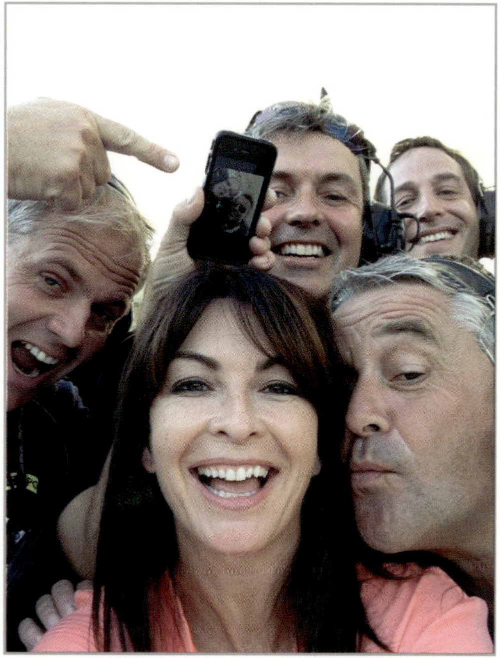

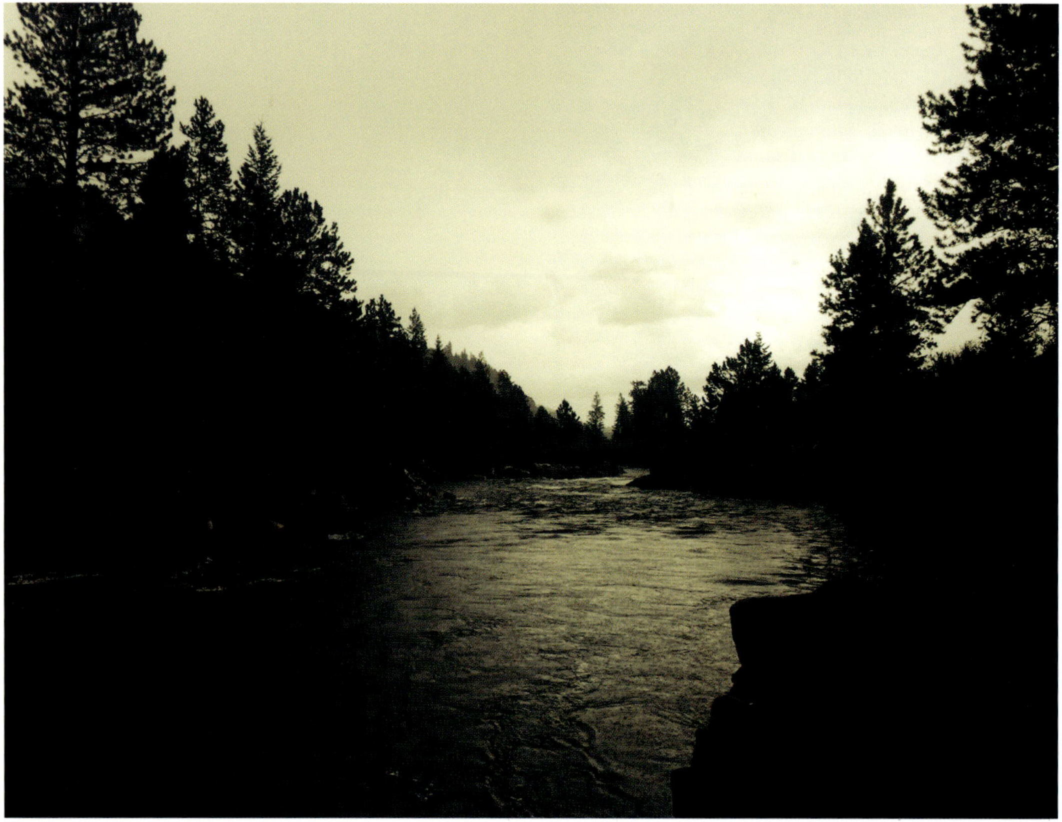

2014 TEAM: MERCEDES

Lewis Hamilton described winning his second world championship in 2014 as "the greatest day of my life." He is now part of an elite group of the most successful drivers in history and is looking to take a third title in 2015.

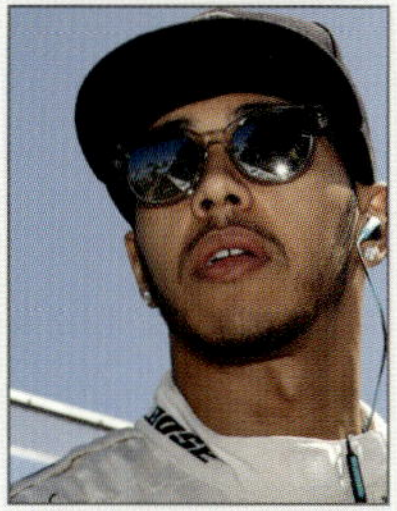

LEWIS HAMILTON

FOLLOW YOUR PATH

"Let life flow like a river, follow the path it takes you down. Take it as it comes and whilst you learn along the way, may you help guide the flow in the direction of your dreams."

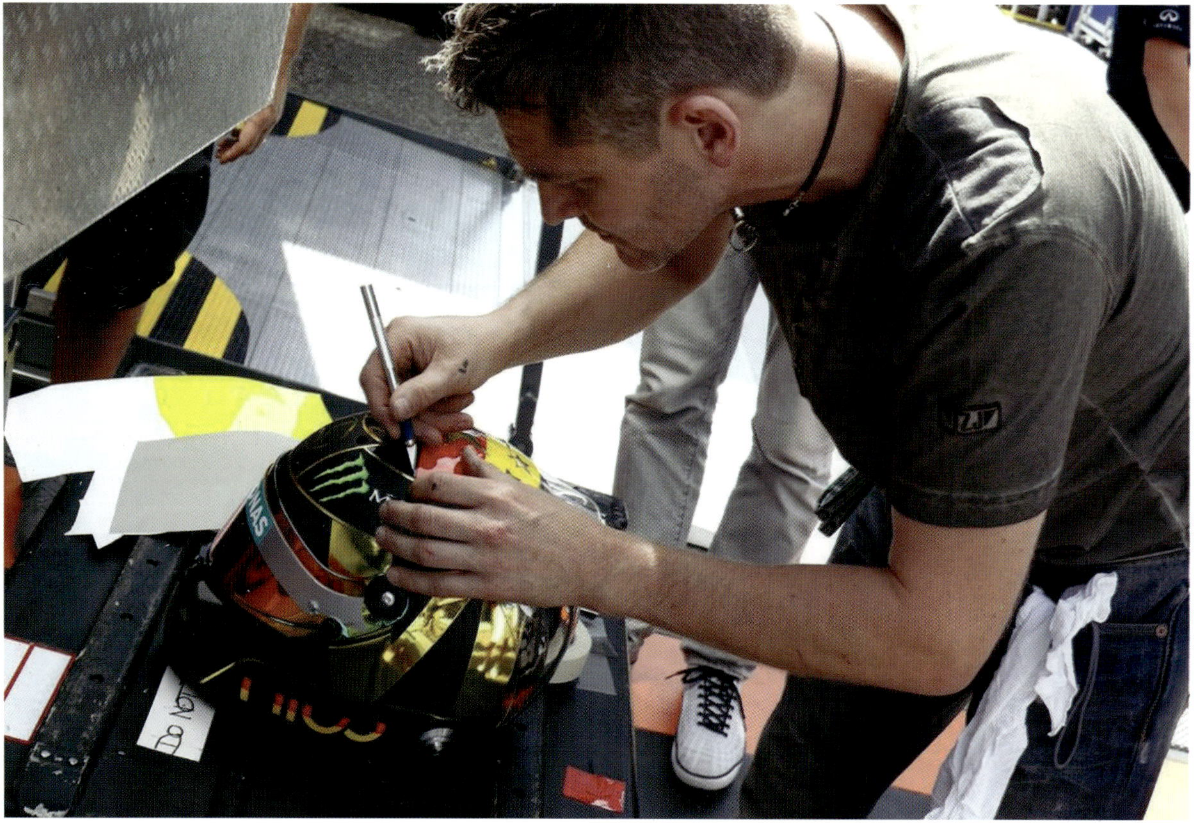

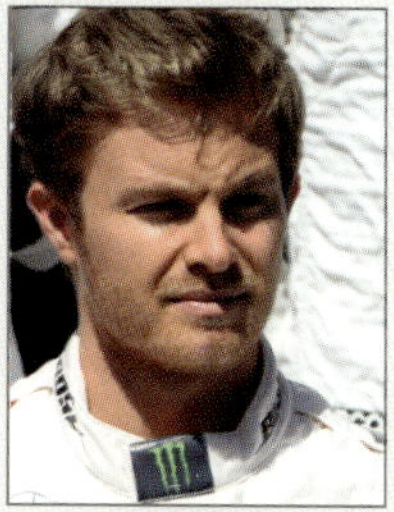

2014 TEAM: MERCEDES

For a large part of the 2014 season it looked like Nico Rosberg might emerge as world champion. After a stunning season-long battle with team-mate Hamilton he had to settle for second, but many believe he will be champion himself one day.

NICO ROSBERG

WORLD CUP HELMET DESIGN

"For the German Grand Prix I just wanted to praise the German National Team with a special German helmet design. I asked my designer Jens Munser to put the World Cup trophy on the top and the famous 4 stars. I loved this helmet design, so I put it on Twitter to show to my fans. I thought, the Trophy belongs to all football fans in the world. But also the FIFA legal office saw my post and asked my management to remove the trophy due to branding rights. We tried to persuade them, but there was no chance. So on Thursday at Hockenheim Jens had to make some changes. He just did the 4 stars a bit bigger and removed the trophy. I was happy with the outcome at the end, because the fourth star nobody can take away from us…"

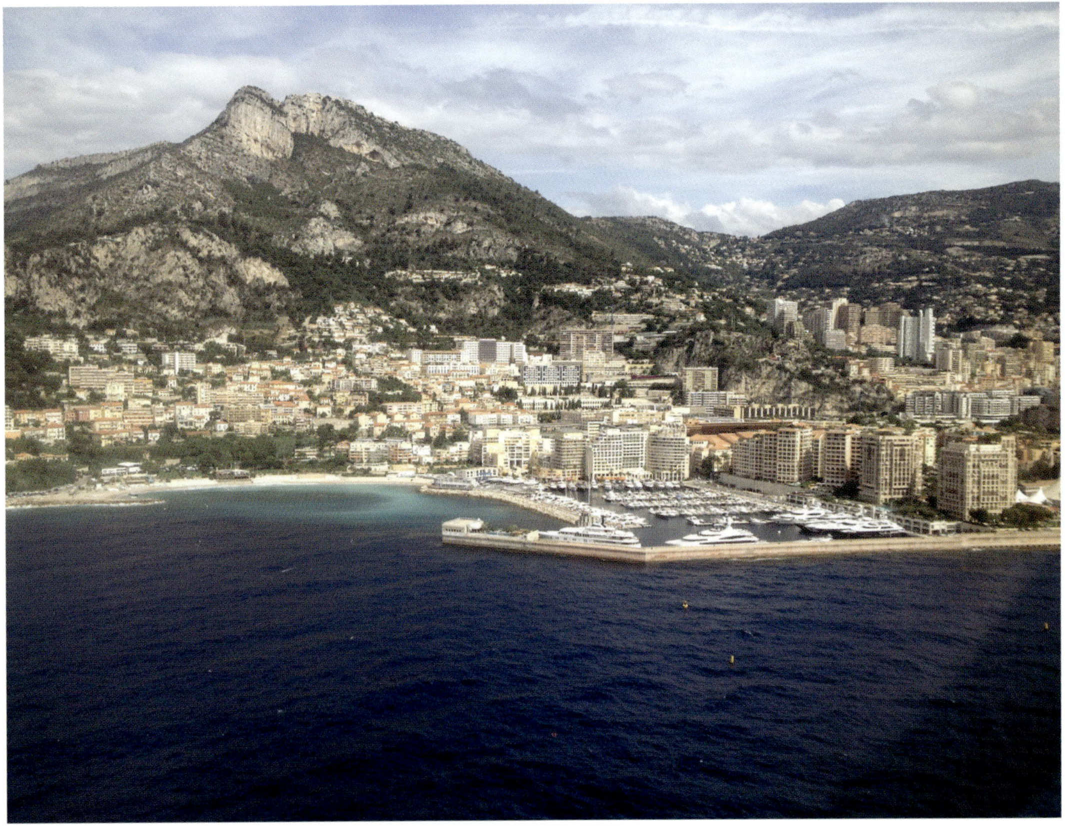

2014 TEAM: RED BULL RACING

In possession of the most famous smile in F1, Daniel Ricciardo finally got his chance to show what he was made of in 2014 when he moved to Red Bull Racing. It was his first time in a top team and he delivered with three victories and many smiles.

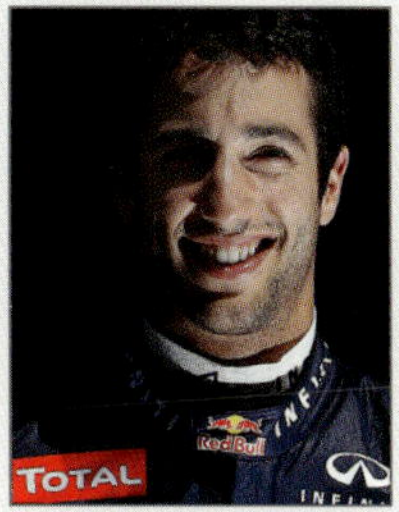

DANIEL RICCIARDO

SEA VIEW

"A view of my new home in Europe. Monaco is a great place for an outdoor lifestyle. Being close to the ocean again is something I've missed."

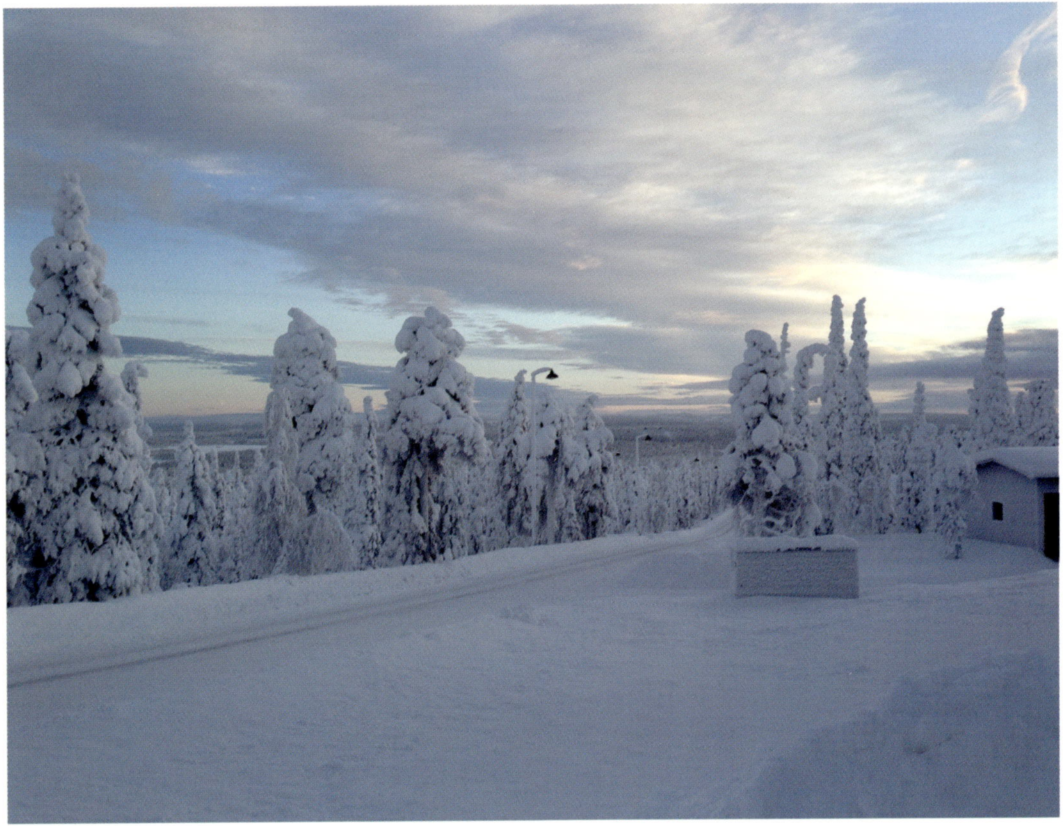

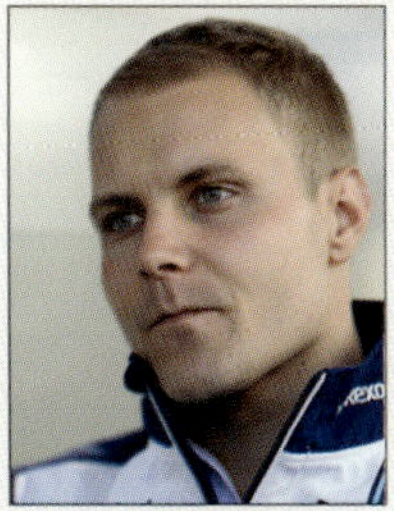

2014 TEAM: WILLIAMS

The latest in a long line of Flying Finns, Valtteri Bottas was many people's surprise driver of the year in 2014. The unassuming Scandinavian took six podiums throughout the season, including back-to-back second places in Britain and Germany.

VALTTERI BOTTAS

CHILLOUT ZONE

"This picture is taken in January in Finnish Lapland. It shows that sometimes it gets pretty cold out there. It also shows how different Finland can be to many other place in the world... I always enjoy to go to these peaceful places."

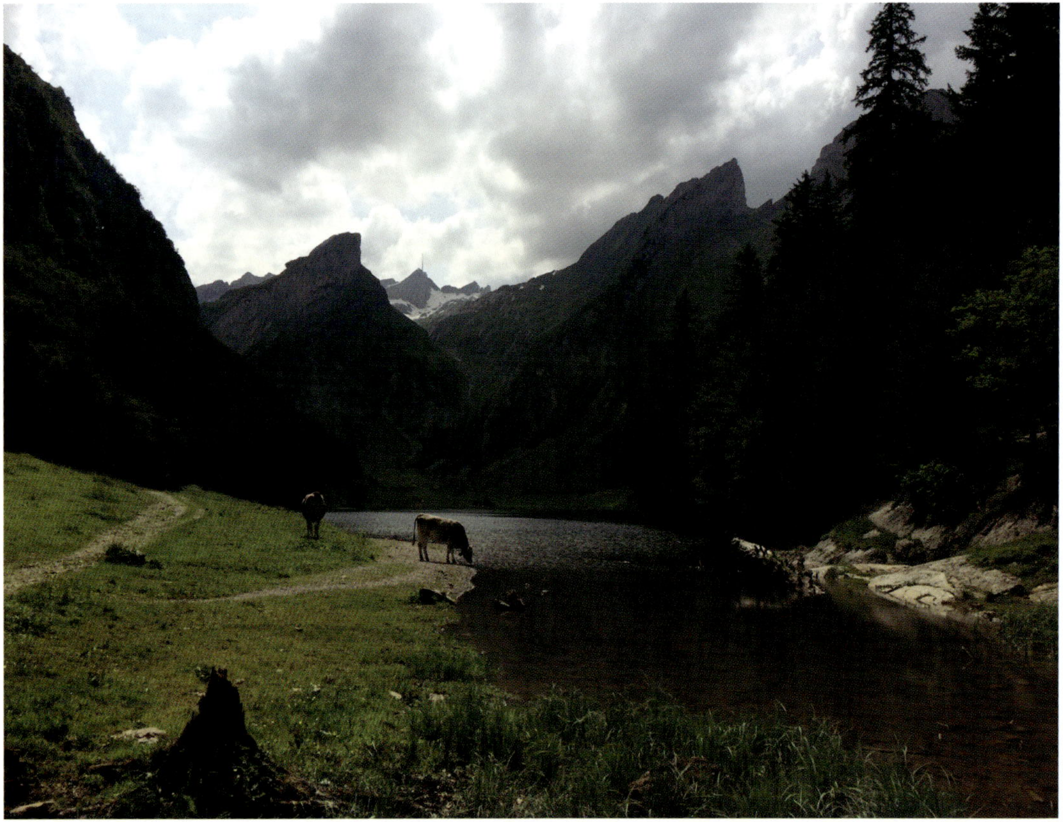

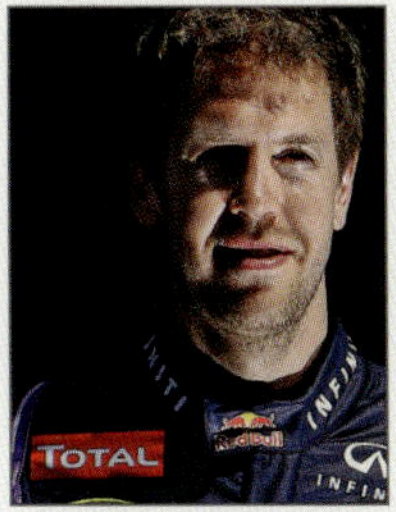

2014 TEAM: RED BULL RACING

Only Michael Schumacher and Juan Manuel Fangio have won more world championships than Sebastian Vettel. Still only 27 at the start of the 2015 season, the quadruple champ has a stack of youthful records: including being the youngest driver to score points, win a race, and take the title.

SEBASTIAN VETTEL

TRAINING IN THE ALPS

"I love the mountains and pure nature. For me it's a perfect surrounding to relax, recharge but of course also to hike and train in fresh clear mountain air. I took this picture in the Alps because it is so peaceful."

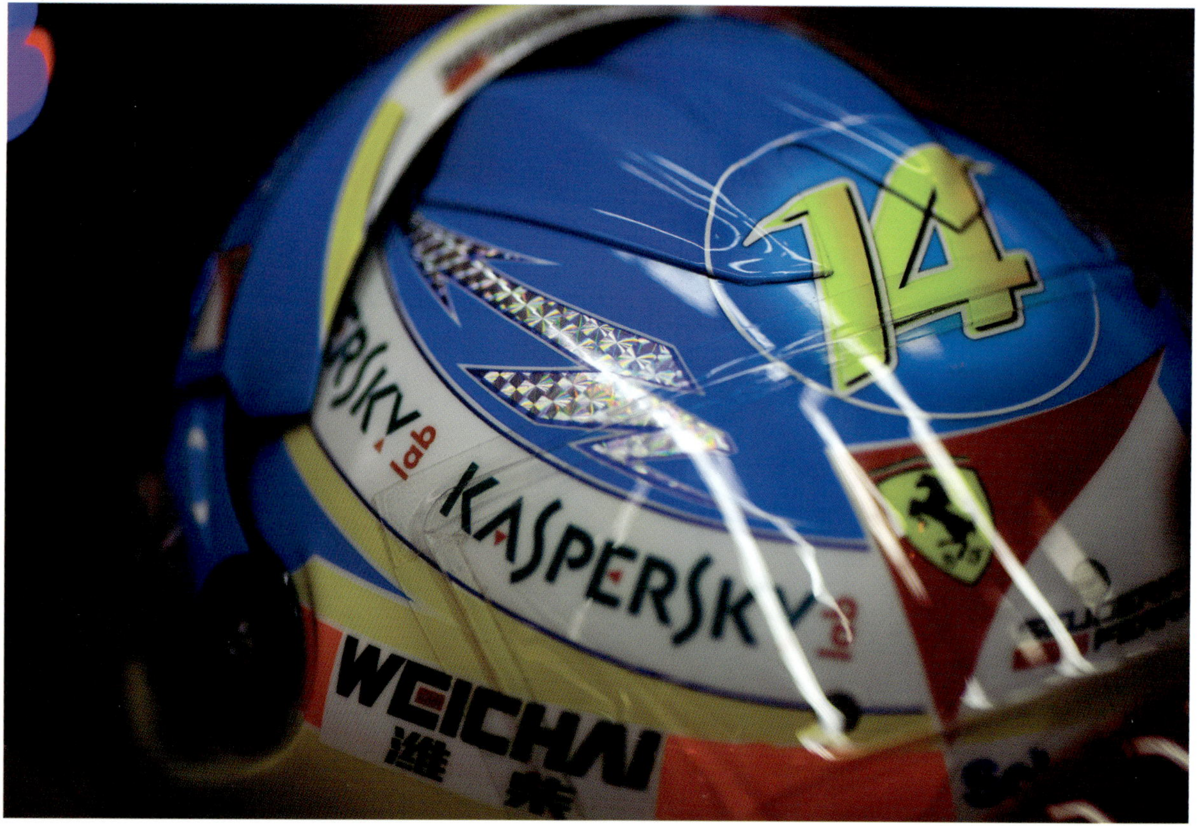
14
KASPERSKY
lab
WEICHAI
潍柴

2014 TEAM: FERRARI

Fernando Alonso is one of the most admired and successful drivers in F1. The Spaniard is one of a rare elite who has won back-to-back titles, in 2005 and 2006. He will be returning to McLaren in 2015 after a seven year absence.

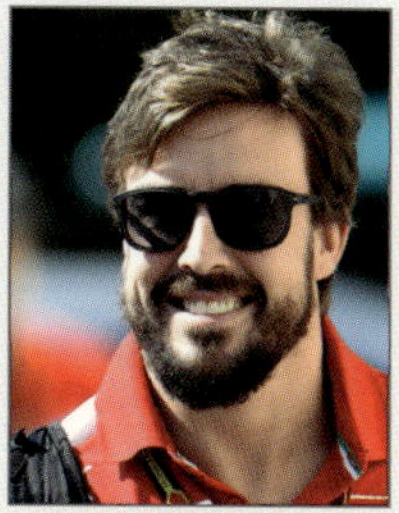

FERNANDO ALONSO

NATIONAL COLOURS

"I change my helmet every year, little differences but always remaining with the blue from my region's flag, Asturias, and then the Spanish flag always somewhere on the helmet."

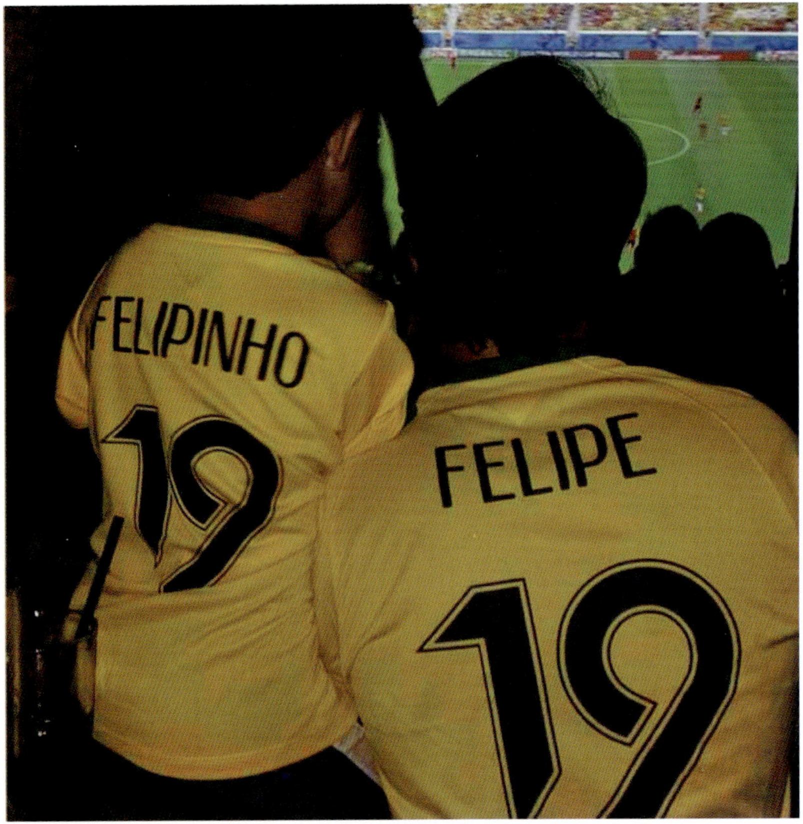
FELIPINHO
19
FELIPE
19

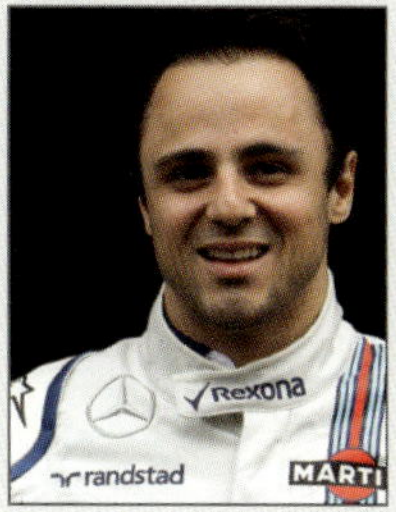

2014 TEAM: WILLIAMS

For many F1 fans, Felipe Massa will always be the man who, for a brief moment in 2008, believed he was world champion. He crossed the line first in the season finale and it looked like he was the victor. However, a last-lap mistake by a rival gave Lewis Hamilton an extra point and the title.

FELIPE MASSA

ME AND MY BOY

"This picture shows how I like to spend my time, watching football. I set my phone on a timer to get me and my son together. He loves football and it's great to be able to watch it with him."

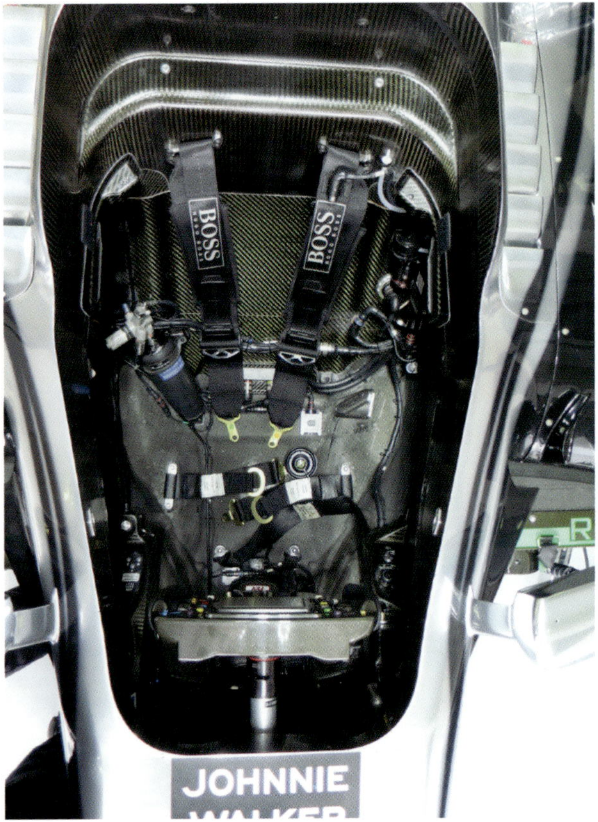
JOHNNIE

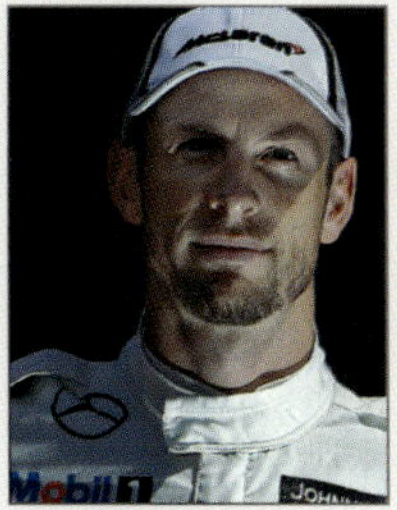

2014 TEAM: MCLAREN

Jenson Button's F1 career has been a rollercoaster ride. Hailed as a great talent on his F1 debut for Williams in 2000, he spent several years in the wilderness, competing in 113 races before he chalked up his first win. He was finally rewarded with the world title in 2009.

JENSON BUTTON

MY OFFICE CHAIR

"I have the best job in the world – and this is my office!"

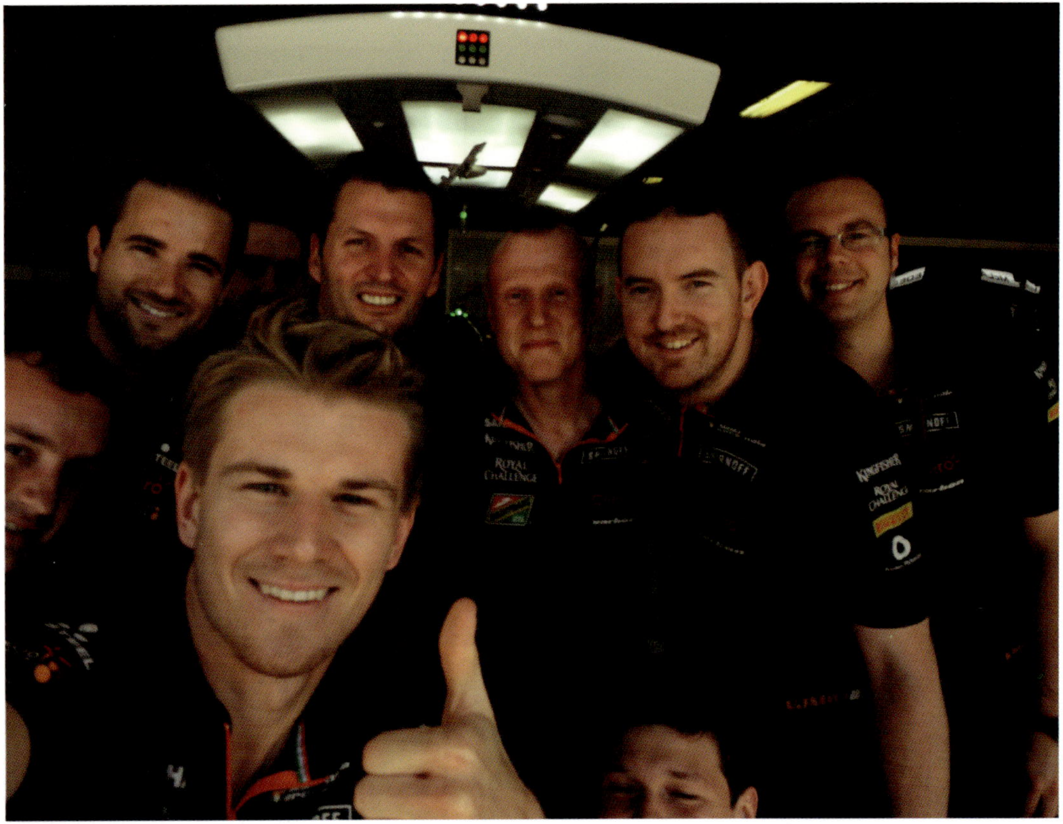

2014 TEAM: FORCE INDIA

Nico Hülkenberg made his Formula One debut for Williams in 2010 when he gained several points finishes and a stunning pole position in a car that was far from the class of the field. Many F1 observers see him as a future race winner.

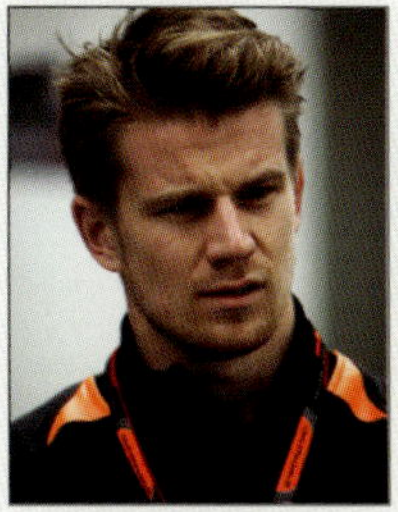

NICO HULKENBERG

YOU NEED A CREW TO GO RACING

"I chose to take a photo of a few of the guys from my car crew. F1 is a true team sport and without these guys I would not be able to go racing. This is just a small selection of the team and everybody plays their part. I took this photo in Budapest on the Thursday morning just before walking the track."

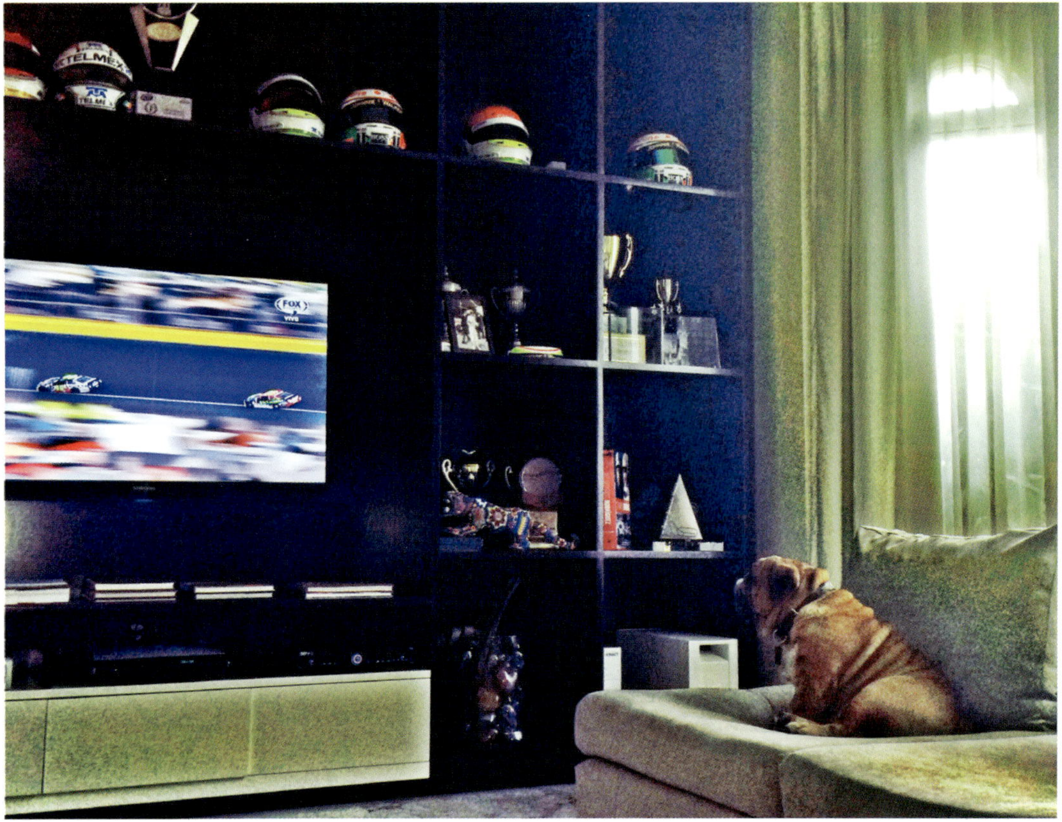
TELMEX
FOX

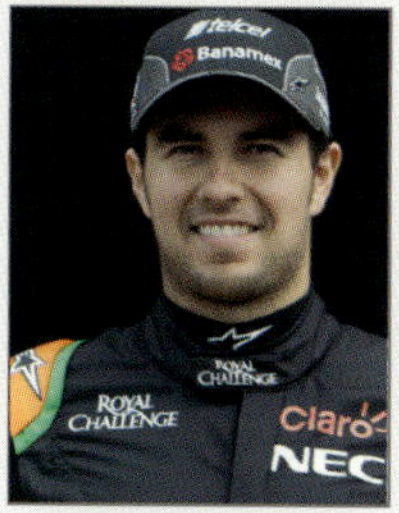

2014 TEAM: FORCE INDIA

Sergio Pérez was hailed as a star of the future when he moved into F1 with Sauber and this was consolidated when he took a stunning second place at the 2012 Malaysian GP. He is a big fan of his bulldog, Canelo, who has featured in all three of his Zoom photos so far.

SERGIO PEREZ

IT'S A DOG'S (DREAM) LIFE

"My dog Canelo watching one of my brother's Nascar races with me. A true fan of motorsport!"

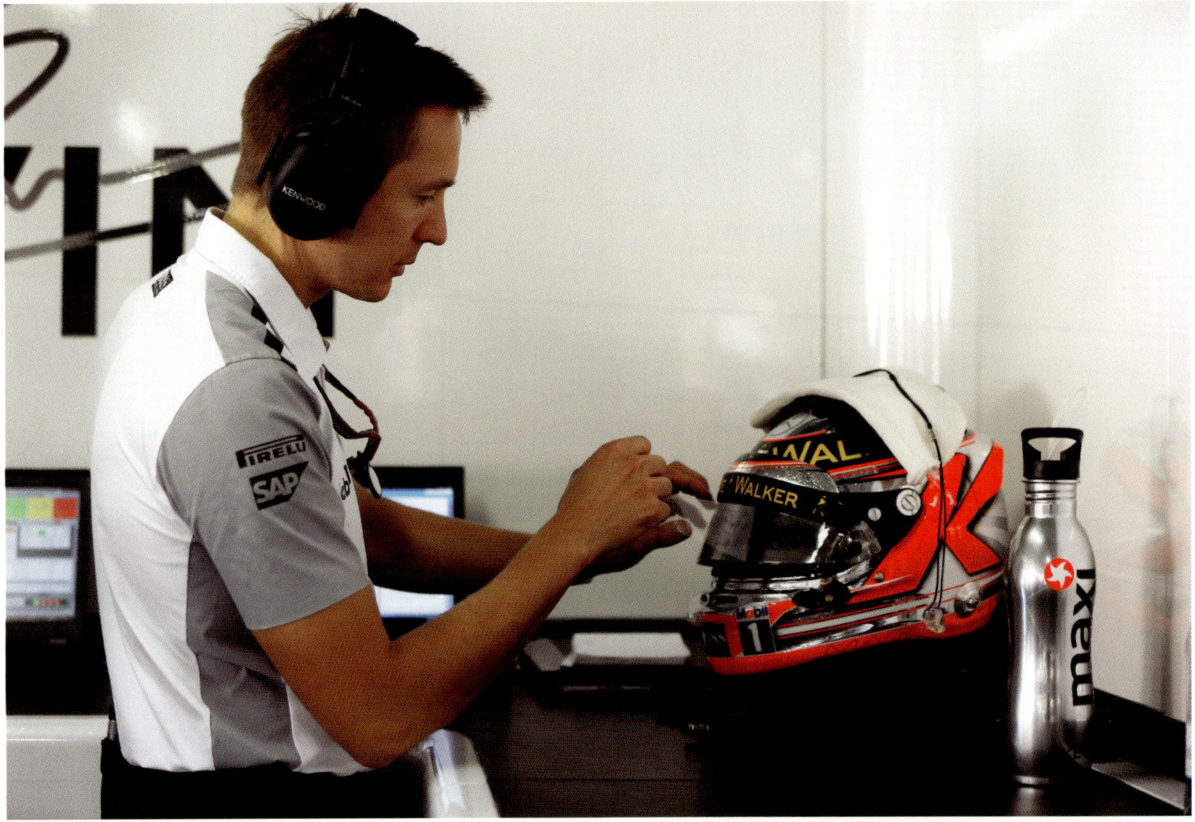
KENWOOD
SAP
WALKER
Mobil
1
maxi

2014 TEAM: MCLAREN

Son of 1990s racer, Jan Magnussen, Kevin followed in his father's footsteps when he joined McLaren at the start of 2014. He immediately impressed with a well-fought second place at the Australian GP, becoming one of a select few drivers to reach the podium on their debut.

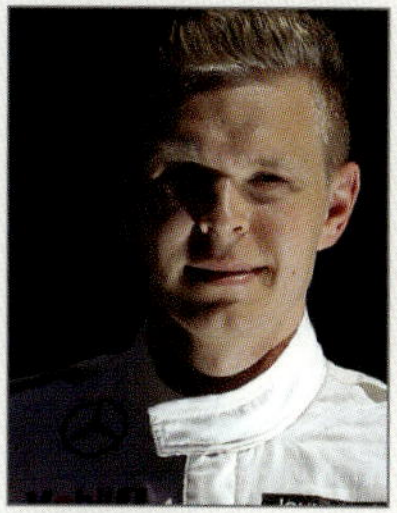

KEVIN MAGNUSSEN

GETTING READY TO RACE

"Antti prepping my helmet."

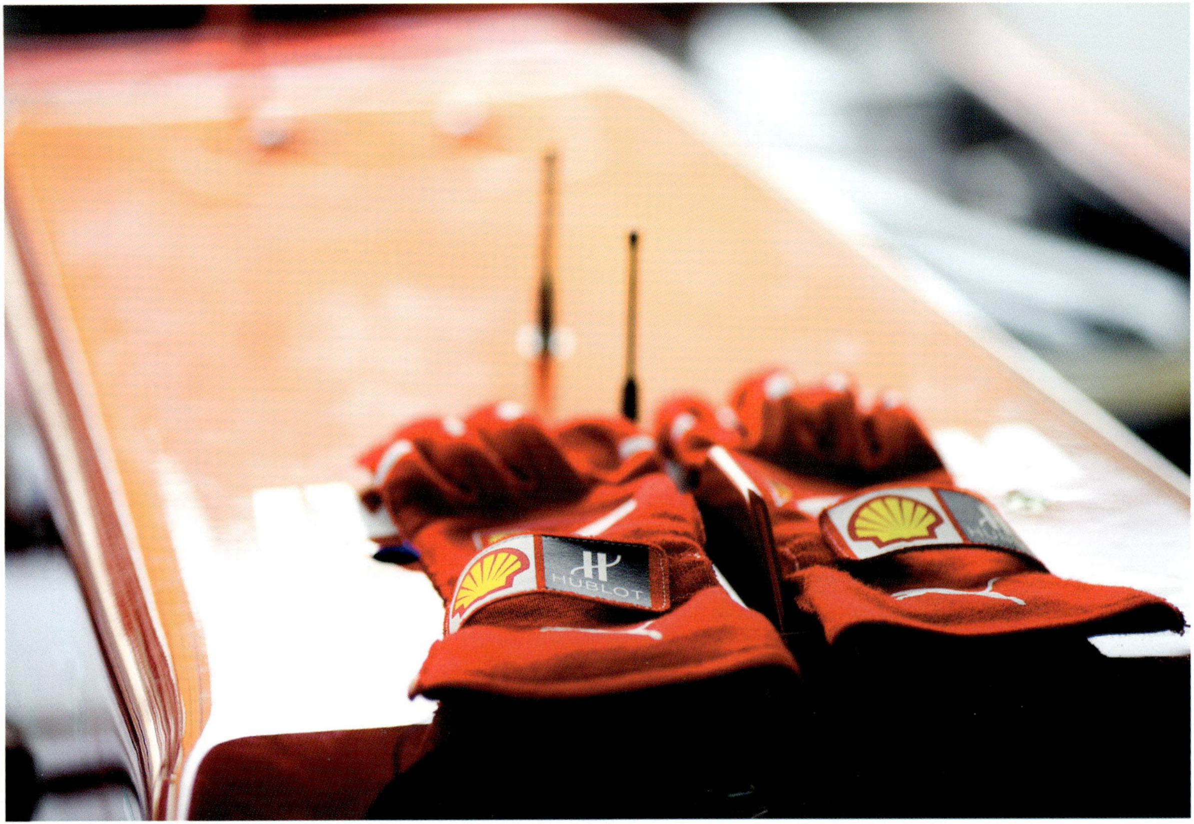
HUBLOT

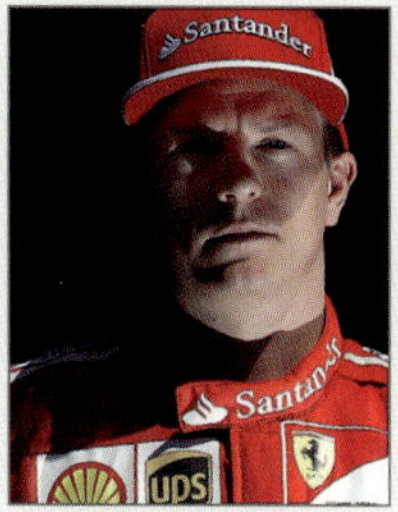

2014 TEAM: FERRARI

'Iceman' Kimi Räikkönen stunned motorsport when he was given his debut F1 drive for Sauber in 2001 after competing in just 23 car races. Despite his doubters he took sixth place in his first race and by 2007 he had become Finland's third world champion.

KIMI RAIKKONEN

READY FOR ACTION

"These are my gloves ready for my return to Ferrari earlier this year. I would rather be in a Ferrari than any other team."

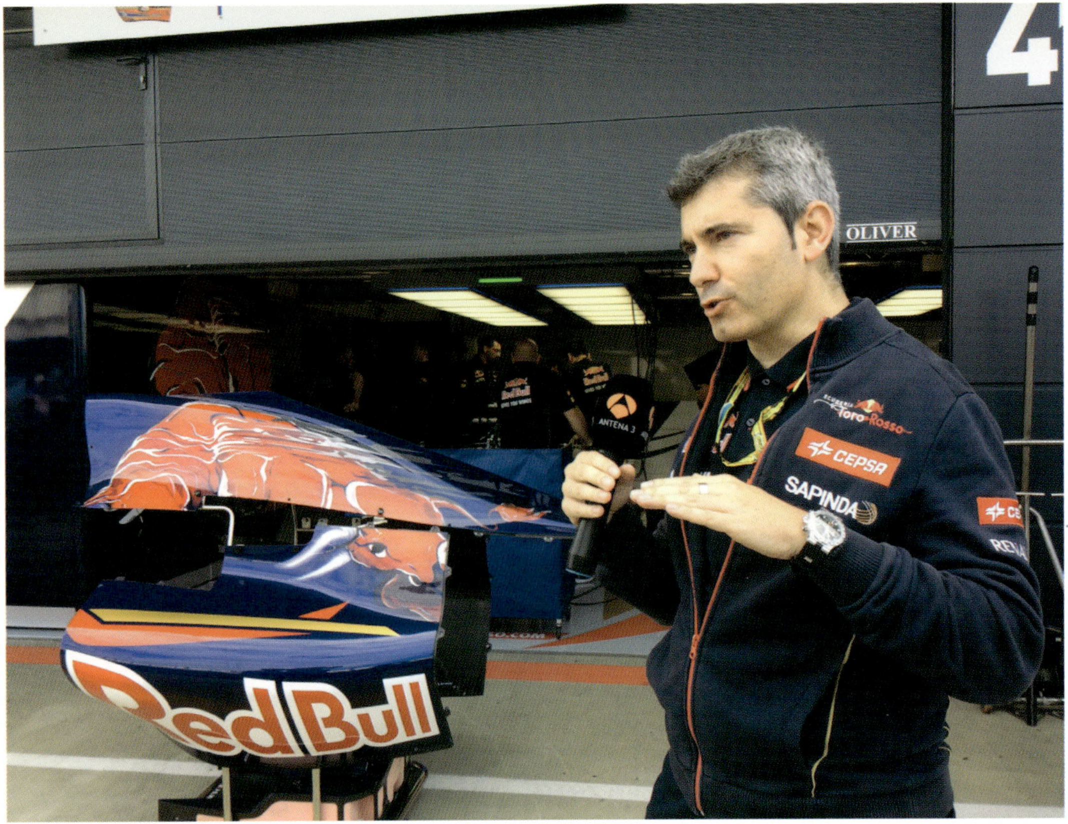
OLIVER
ANTENA 3
Scuderia Toro Rosso
CEPSA
SAPINDA
Red Bull

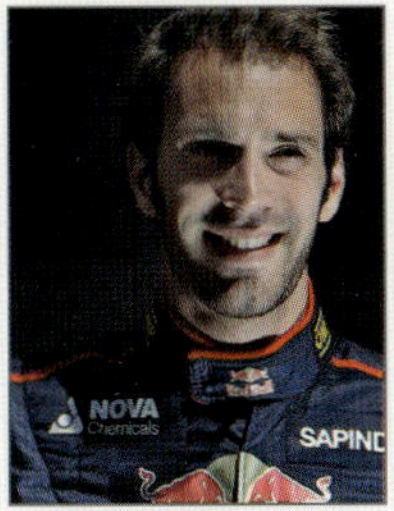

2014 TEAM: TORO ROSSO

Jean-Éric Vergne made his debut for Toro Rosso at the 2012 Australian GP and scored his first points at the following round in Malaysia. He has recently become one of the stars of the new FIA Formula E series and will combine this with a role as Ferrari's test driver in 2015.

JEAN-ERIC VERGNE

KEEP CALM AND RACE ON

"This is my race engineer Javier Pujolar. I took the photo while waiting for him to finish an interview with Spanish TV before we went to do our pre-race weekend track walk at the Austrian Grand Prix. Apart from Fernando Alonso, there are not that many Spanish people in the F1 paddock, so Xevi, as everyone calls him, is in big demand with the Spanish media. He takes it all in his stride, as he is very a calm person, a characteristic which is very useful for a race engineer, as it's a very high pressure job. We have only worked together since the start of this year. He is very experienced and I have learned a lot from him about how to get the most out of the race car and we have a really nice relationship."

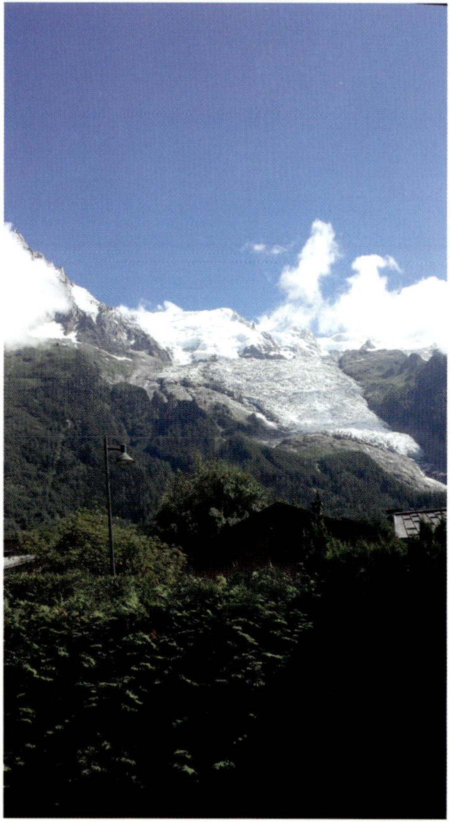

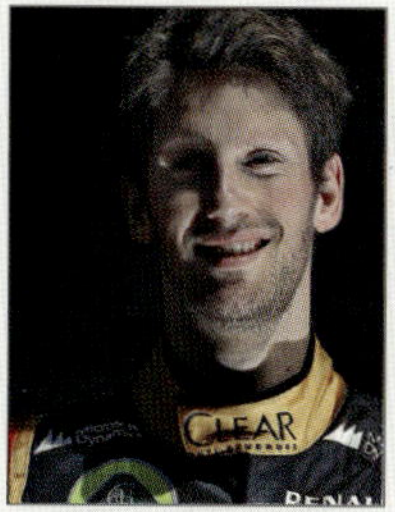

2014 TEAM: LOTUS

After a patchy first season in 2009, few observers expected to see Romain Grosjean in F1 again. However, Lotus took a chance in 2012 and the Frenchman delivered one stunning performance after another, making him a firm fan favourite and establishing him as a future star of the sport.

ROMAIN GROSJEAN

ABSENT FRIENDS

"This picture carries a lot of meaning for me. It is the view from the chalet in the Alps, in Chamonix, where I spent my first holiday with my wife Marion and where my best man (who sadly died on the 29th of July 2014) used to live."

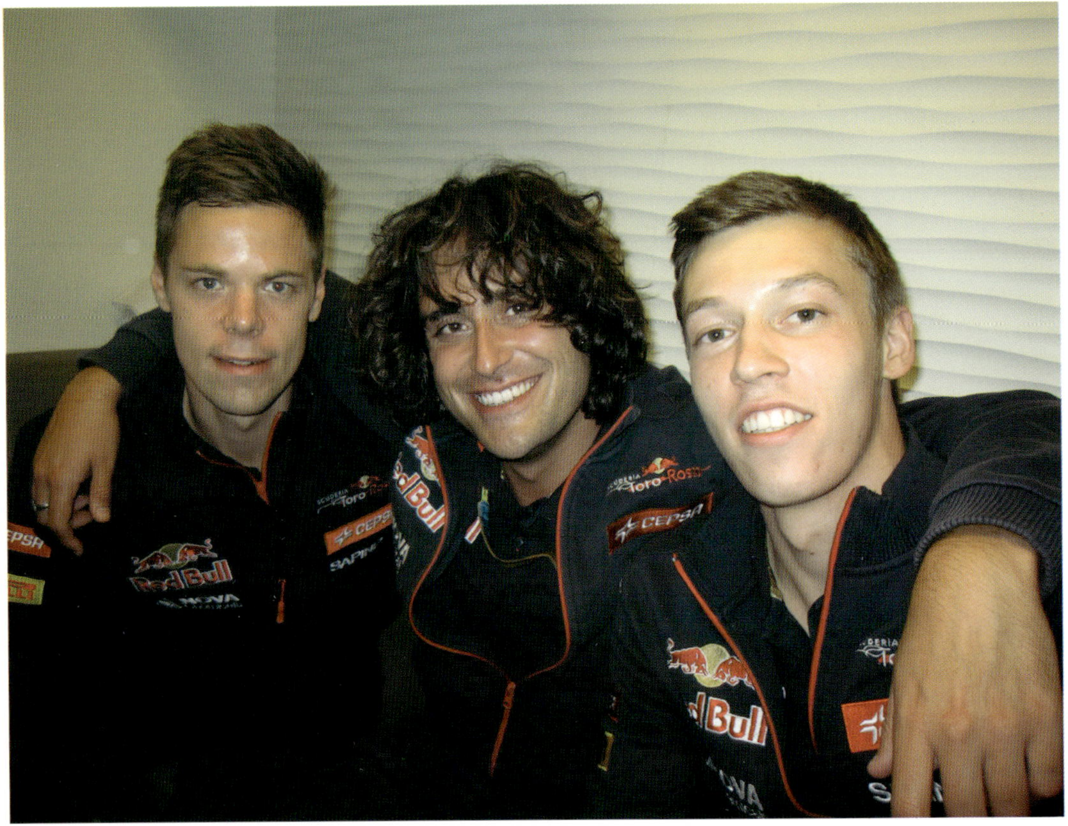
Red Bull
CEPSA
Toro Rosso

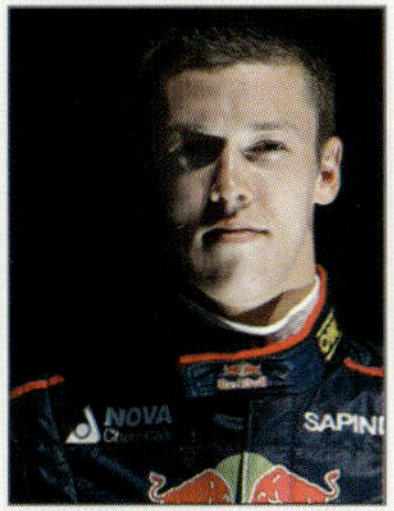

2014 TEAM: TORO ROSSO

Only the second Russian to race in F1, Daniil Kvyat broke Sebastian Vettel's record for being F1's youngest points scorer when he finished 9th on his debut as a 19-year-old at the start of 2014. His performance was enough to earn him a seat with Red Bull Racing for 2015.

DANIIL KVYAT

THREE'S NOT A CROWD

"These are the people I spend the most time with in my working life, my race engineer Marco Matassa and my trainer Pyry Salmela. We are like a small team within the Toro Rosso team. This particular photo was taken on Thursday evening in Spa. We were in a good mood, as we always are, to be honest. I get on well with Pyry and also with my engineer Marco and with him, it helps that I can speak Italian as well. We have a lot of fun but more importantly, we all enjoy a good working relationship."

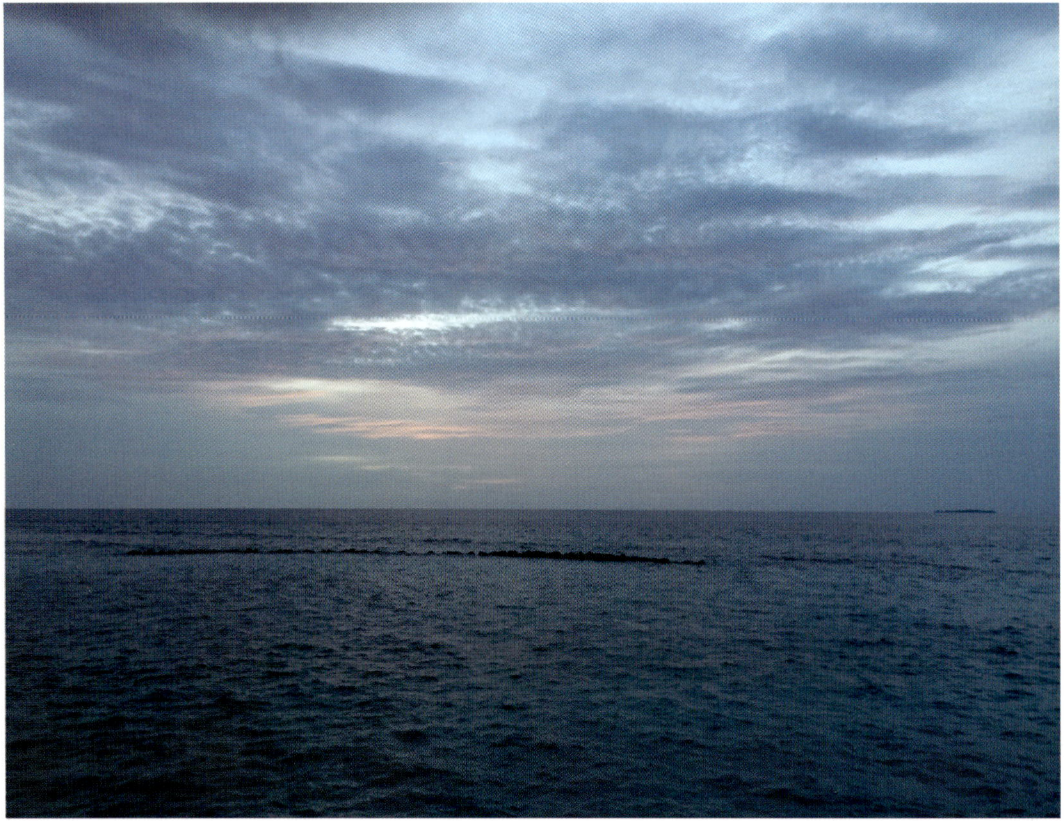

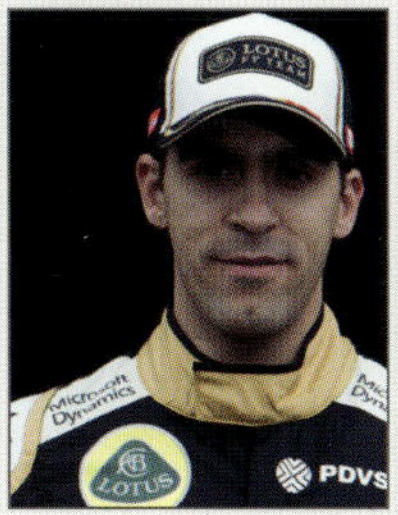

2014 TEAM: LOTUS

When Pastor Maldonado first entered F1 in 2011 there were many observers who saw him as a pay driver and doubted he was the right man for the job. However, all that was put behind him when he surged to victory in the 2012 Spanish GP, the first win for Williams in almost eight years.

PASTOR MALDONADO

LOS ROQUES

"This picture was taken by me in Los Roques, Venezuela. 'Sunset'."

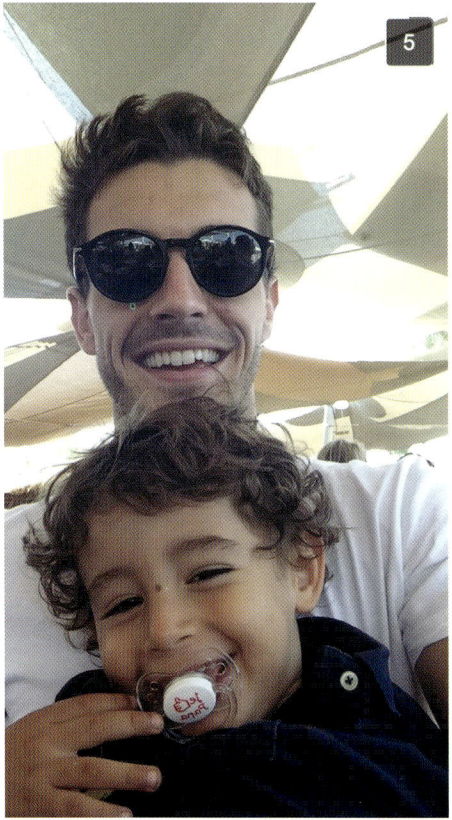
5

2014 TEAM: MARUSSIA

Jules Bianchi was born into a racing family. His talent was spotted by Ferrari back in 2009 when they gave the then 20-year-old Frenchman a test drive. He graduated to F1 with Marussia in 2013, scoring the team's only points at the 2014 Monaco Grand Prix before his season was cut short by his devastating accident at Suzuka.

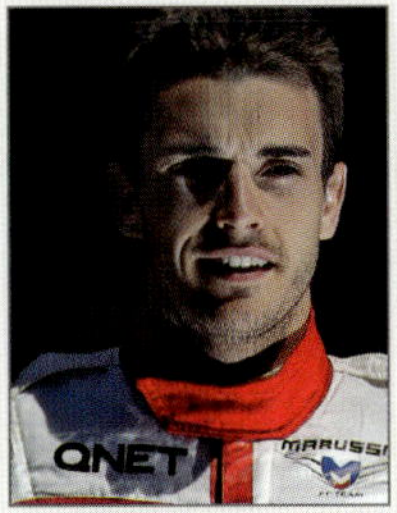

JULES BIANCHI

Jules Bianchi took this selfie for Zoom in September 2014. Unfortunately, Jules' crash at Suzuka took place before he was able to sign it, so it did not appear in our auction earlier this year, however the Bianchi family has kindly given us permission to feature the photograph in this book. We would like to thank Jules for all the support he has given to the Zoom project and Great Ormond Street Hospital Children's Charity. #ForzaJules

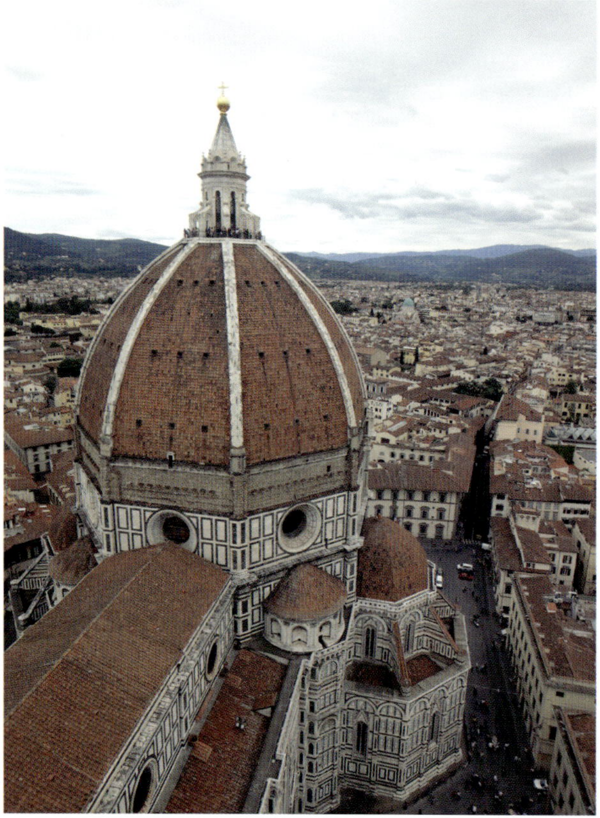

2014 TEAM: SAUBER

Adrian Sutil made his Formula One debut in 2007 for the Spyker team and scored the only point of the team's brief F1 career at the Japanese GP. Since then he has been a solid presence in the sport who is known to be able deliver the goods.

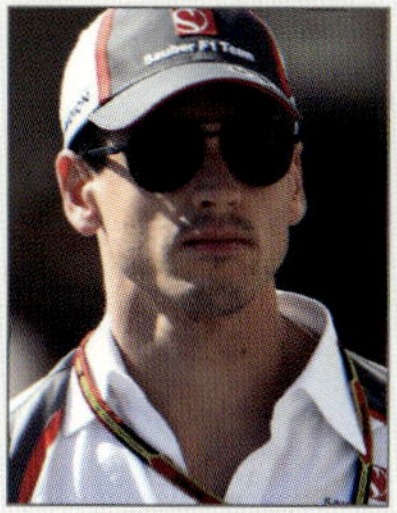

ADRIAN SUTIL

FABULOUS FLORENCE

"This picture was taken in Florence. The city is one of the most beautiful places I have been to. As I like a lot the culture from different countries and especially from Italy, it is a place I really love to go."

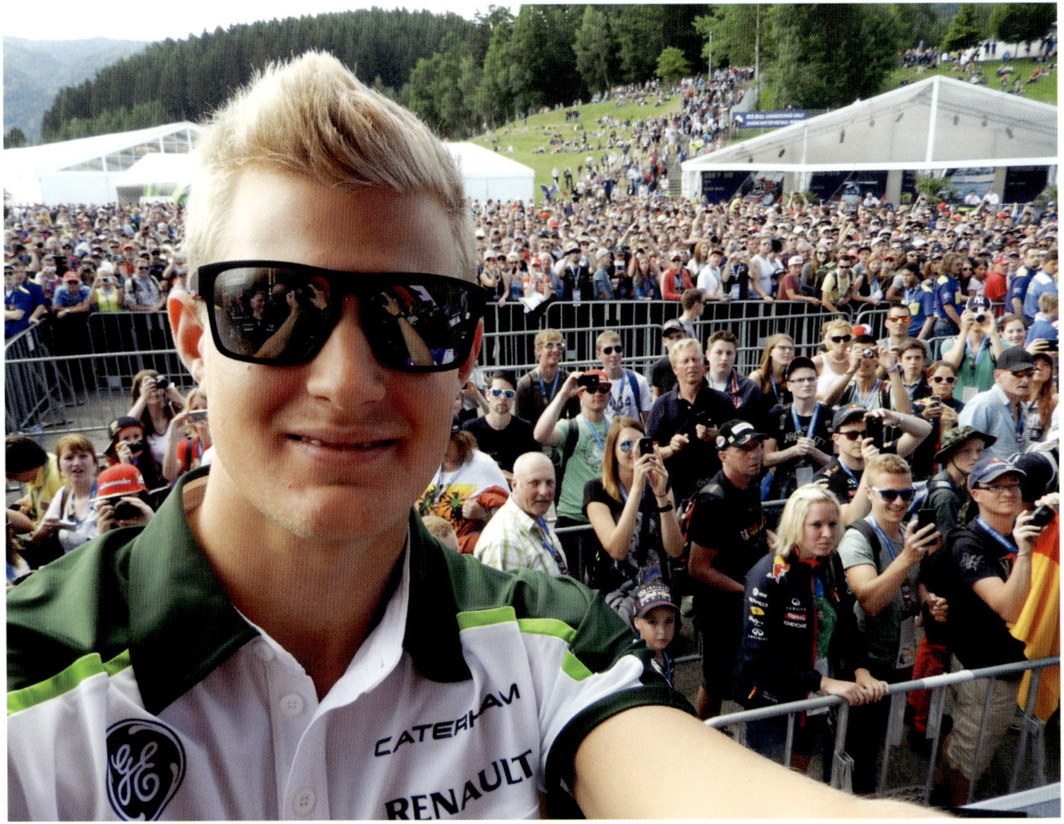
CATERHAM
RENAULT

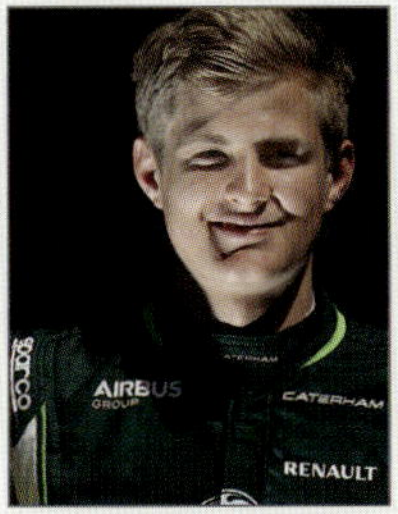

2014 TEAM: CATERHAM

Sweden's Marcus Ericsson is a former GP2 winner who made his debut for Caterham in 2014. Despite a tough season at the struggling outfit, he just missed out on scoring points in Monaco and he has been signed by Sauber for 2015.

MARCUS ERICSSON

FAN EXPERIENCE

"Selfie with the fans at the Austrian Grand Prix autograph session - an amazing experience."

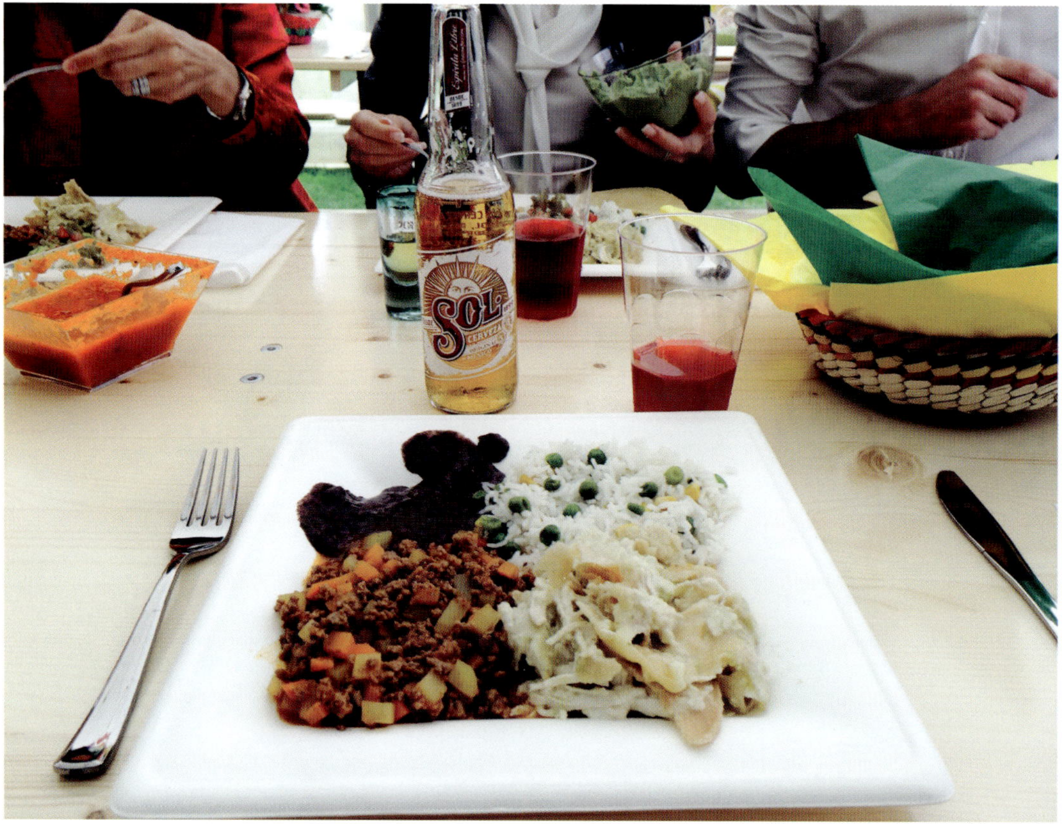
SOL
CERVEZA

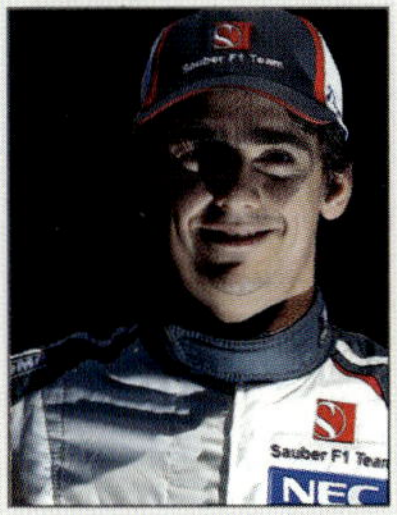

2014 TEAM: SAUBER

Mexico's Esteban Gutiérrez came to F1 as a rookie in 2013, with an impressive record in junior formulae. He scored his first points at the Japanese GP that year with an impressive drive to seventh place and has earned himself a role as a Ferrari test driver in 2015.

ESTEBAN GUTIERREZ

HOME FROM HOME

"This picture is special. I had this Mexican meal in Switzerland. I have been living in Switzerland for 1.5 years and it was probably the first proper Mexican food I had lately."

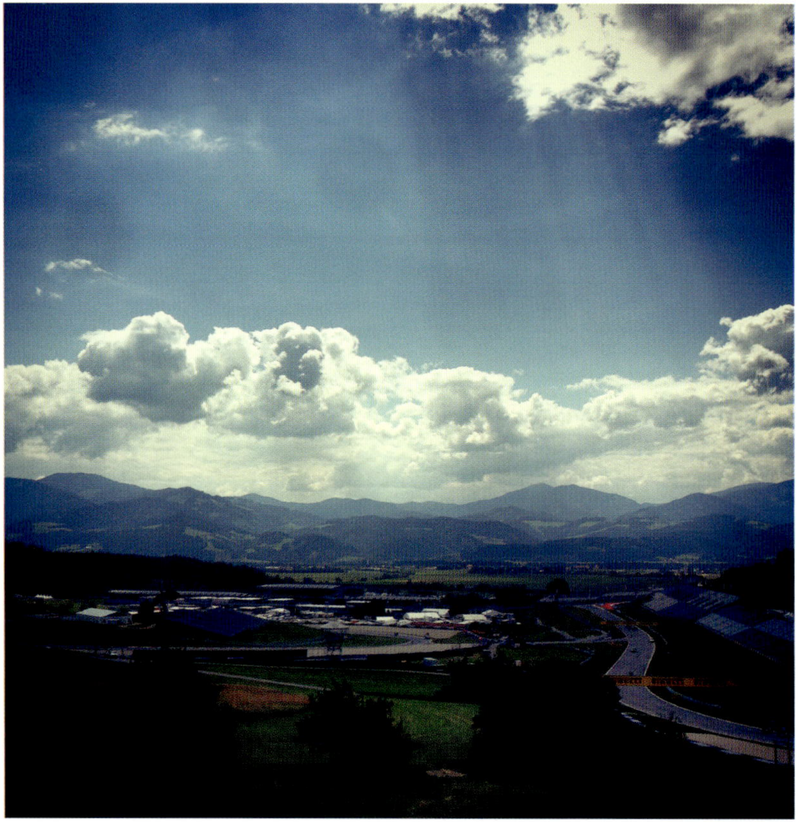

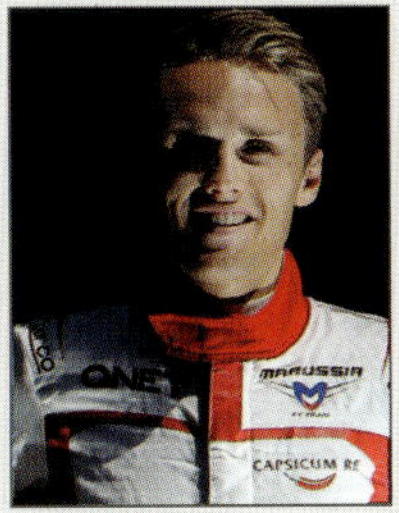

2014 TEAM: MARUSSIA

Max Chilton is the latest in a long line of British racing drivers to make it to the wheel of an F1 car. He made his debut for Marussia in 2013 and although he didn't have a chance to fight the big names he impressed in other ways, becoming the first driver in history to make it to the finish line in his first 17 races.

MAX CHILTON

TRACK LANDSCAPE

"A view of the mountains."

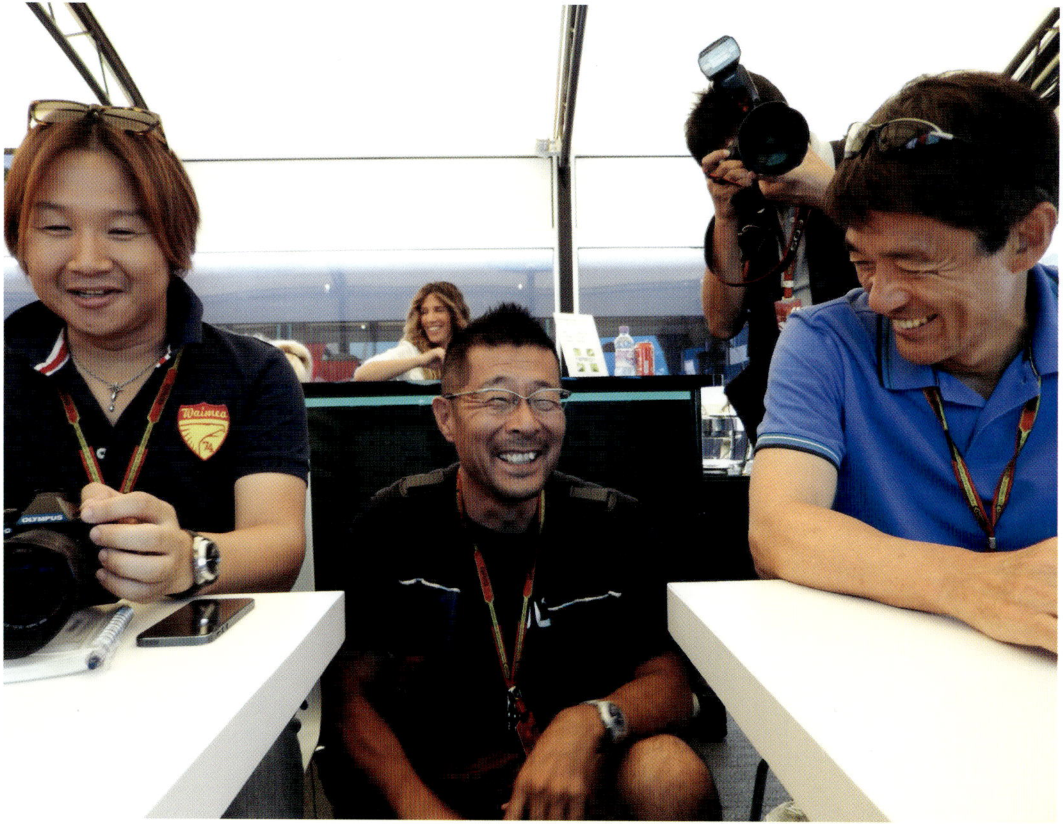
Waimea
OLYMPUS

2014 TEAM: CATERHAM

Kamui Kobayashi made his F1 debut with Toyota at the 2009 Japanese GP where, to the surprise of many, he fought with Jenson Button for several laps. Button jokingly described him as "absolutely crazy" and since then he has been widely praised for his aggressive style and overtaking ability.

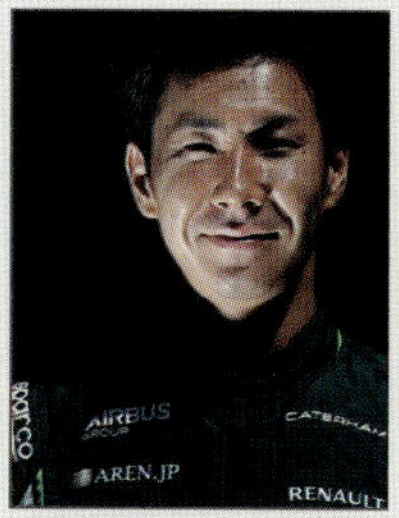

KAMUI KOBAYASHI

MY VERY OWN MEDIA TEAM

"Japanese media, the people I see at every race."

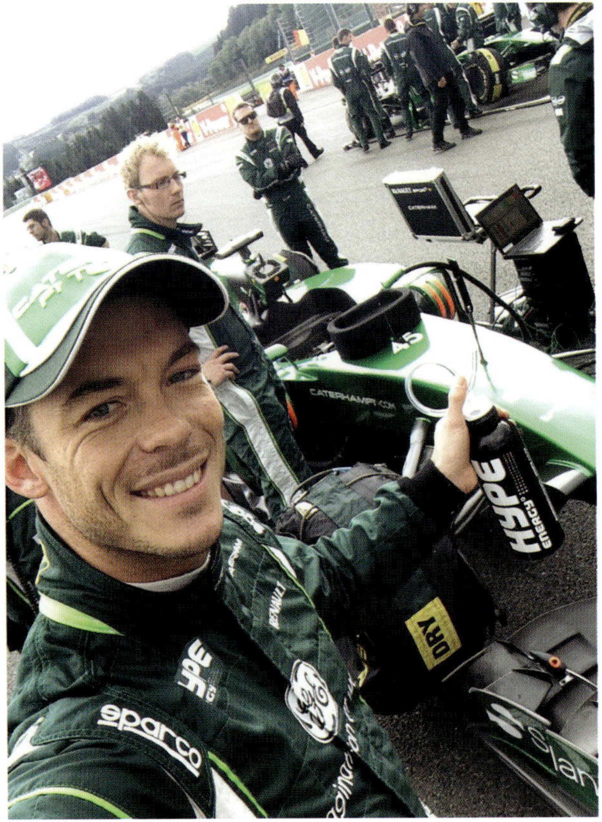
sparco
HYPE
ENERGY
DRY

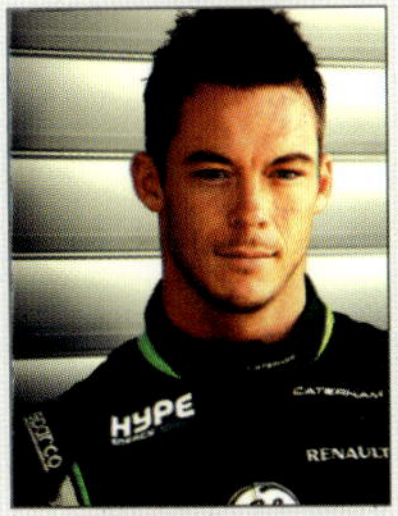

2014 TEAM: CATERHAM

It looked like three-times Le Mans winner Andre Lotterer would be confined to the long list of talented drivers who had never made it to F1. However, that changed at the 2014 Belgian GP when he finally made his F1 debut at the age of 32 for Caterham.

ANDRE LOTTERER

ME IN SPA

"Selfie in Spa-Francorchamps."

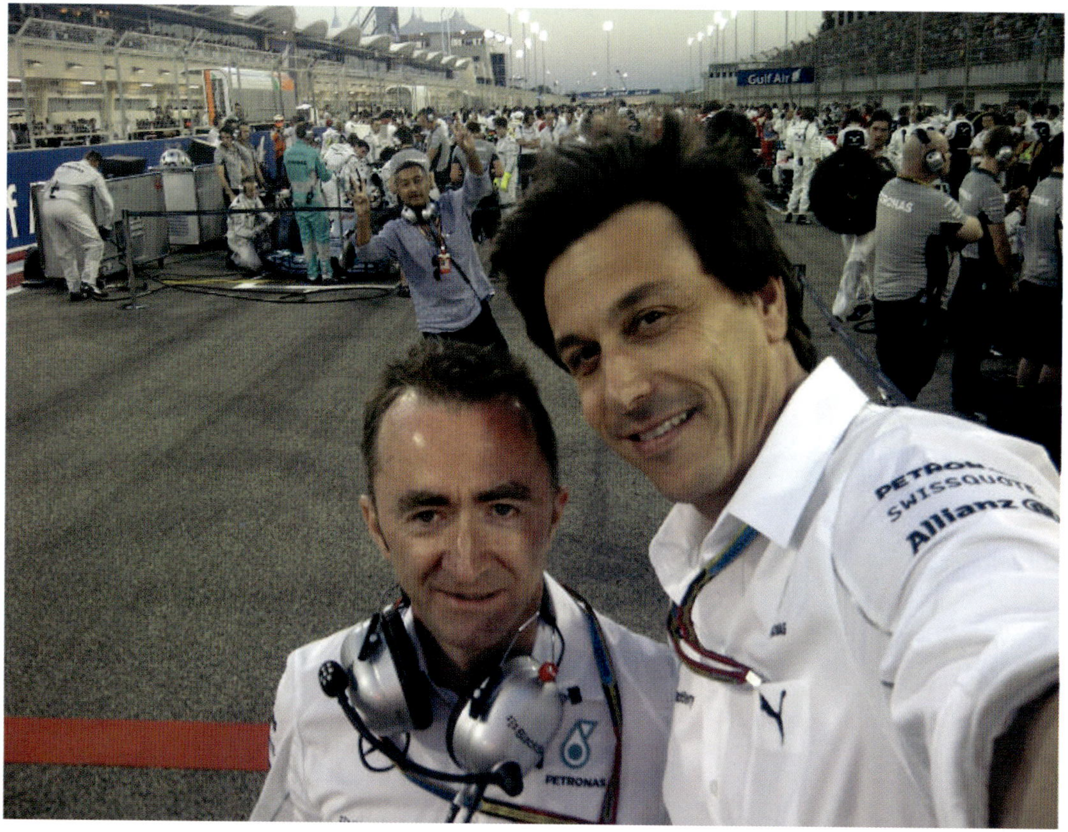
Gulf Air
SWISSQUOTE
Allianz
PETRONAS

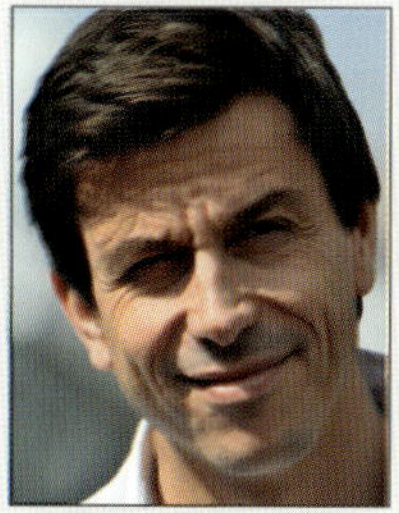

TEAM: MERCEDES

Toto Wolff started out in motorsport as a driver but he also set up an investment company, which first put money into German racing team HWA and then Williams in 2009. In 2013, he became executive director at the Mercedes team, acquiring a 30% stake. He is married to Williams test driver, Susie Wolff.

TOTO WOLFF

PHOTOBOMBER

"It's a selfie from the most dramatic race of the year, Bahrain, and has a rather prominent photobomber – the promoter of the Malaysian GP!"

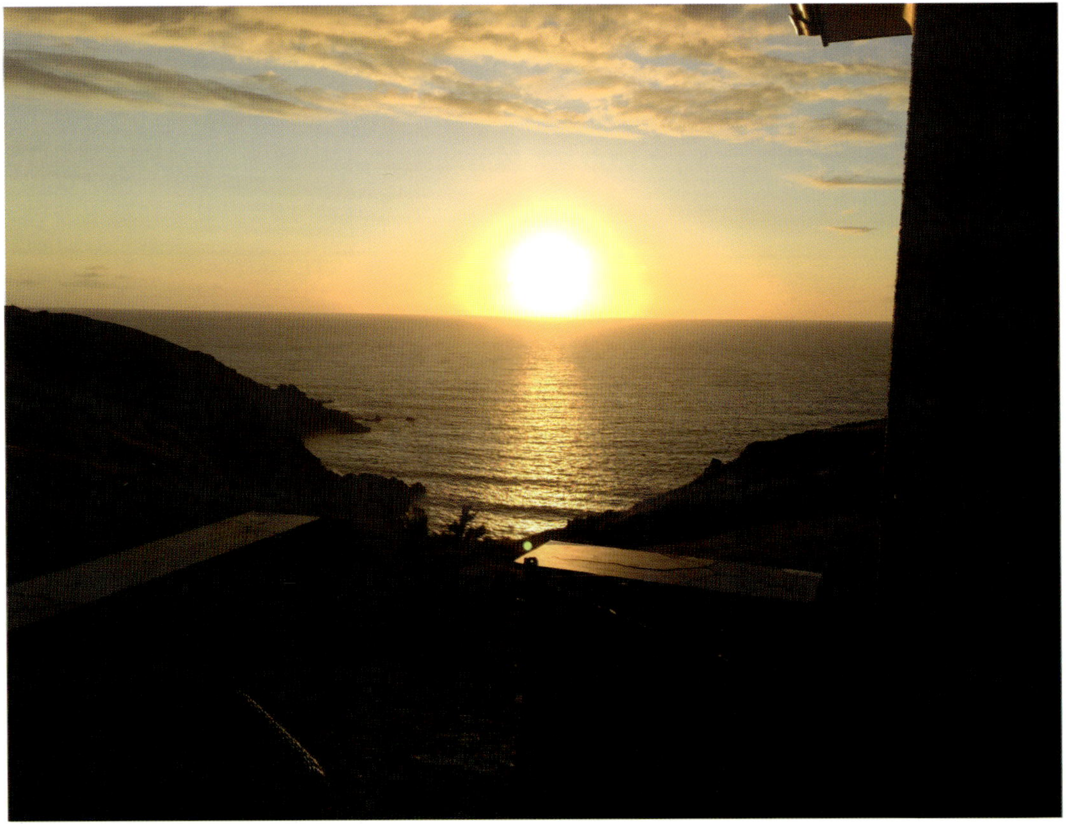

TEAM: RED BULL RACING

Christian Horner was a championship-winning boss in Formula 3000 when his skills caught the eye of Red Bull boss, Dietrich Mateschitz, who put him in charge of Red Bull Racing. Horner led the team to both drivers' and constructors' world championships for four years in a row from 2010 and 2013.

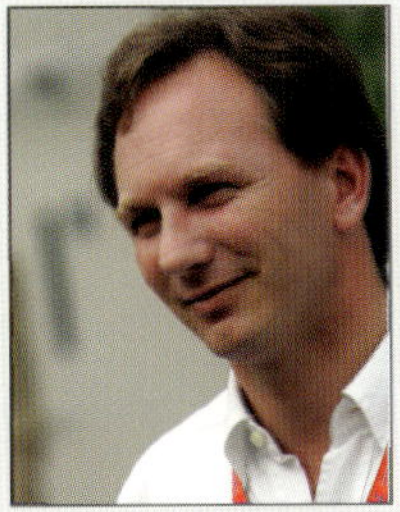

CHRISTIAN HORNER

CORNISH HOLIDAYS

"This is in Cornwall, which is one of the places I like to go on holiday."

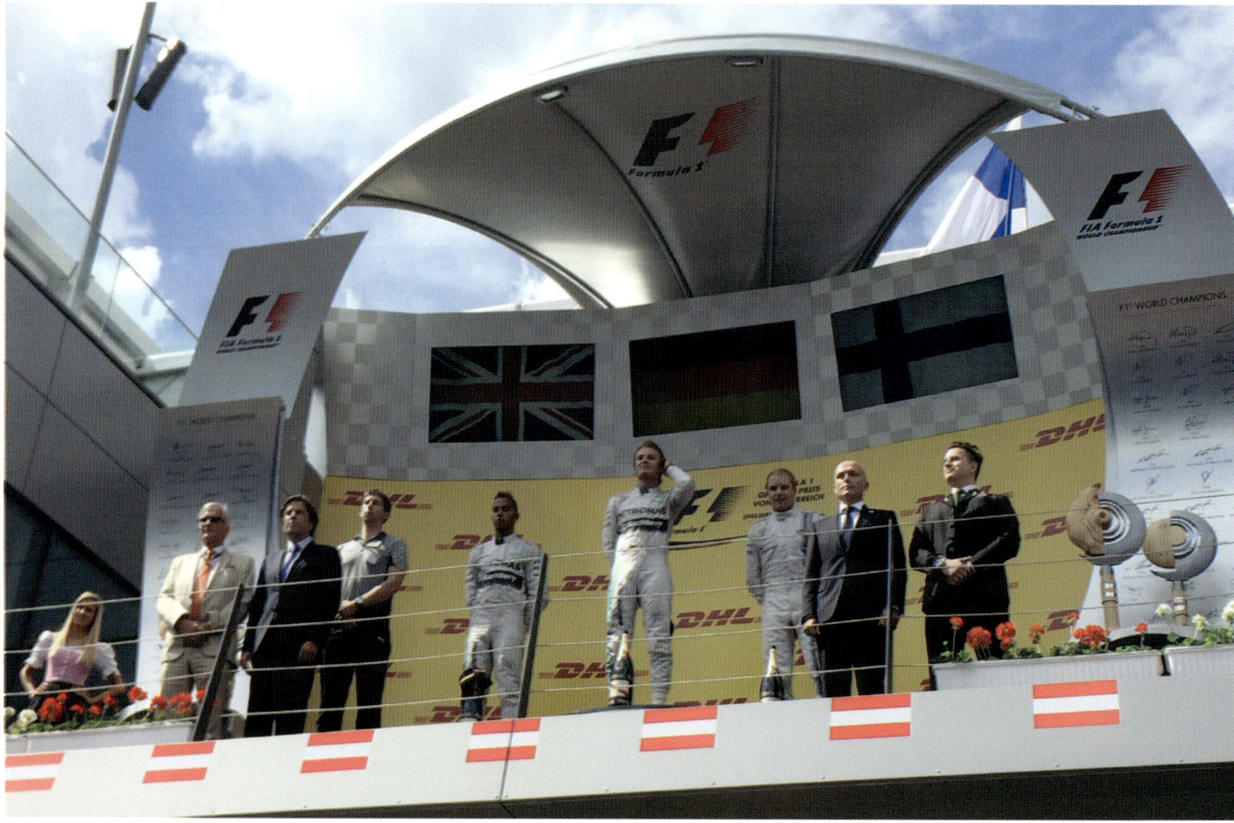
Formula 1
FIA Formula 1
FIA Formula 1
F1 WORLD CHAMPIONS
DHL

TEAM: WILLIAMS

As the daughter of Williams' founder Sir Frank, Claire Williams has racing in her blood. She has followed in the family footsteps since she left university when her first job was as a press officer at Silverstone. She joined the family business the following year. She was appointed deputy team principal in 2013.

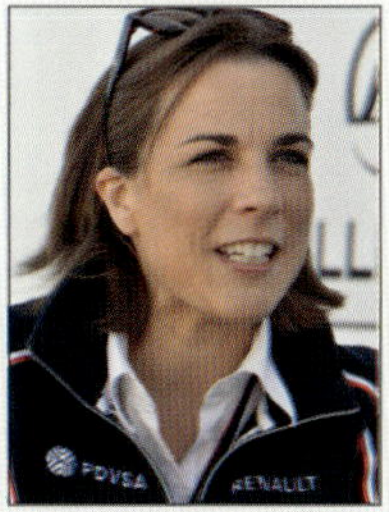

CLAIRE WILLIAMS

PERFECT PODIUMS

"The podium in Austria, our first this year and also Valtteri's first podium in F1."

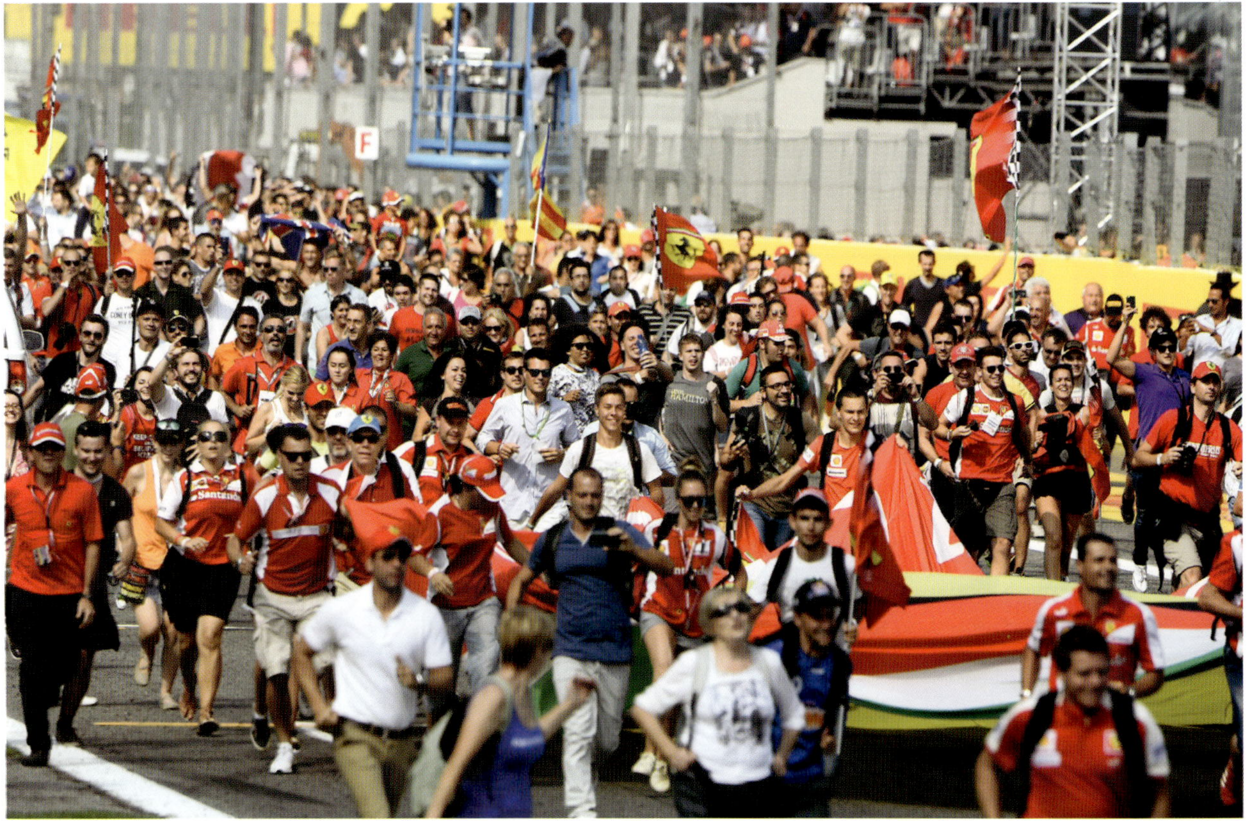
F

TEAM: FERRARI

Although he only became Ferrari team principal at the end of the 2014 season, Maurizio Arrivabene already has a long history in F1. As the marketing head of Ferrari partner Philip Morris, he got to know the team well and has sat on the F1 Commission as a sponsor representative.

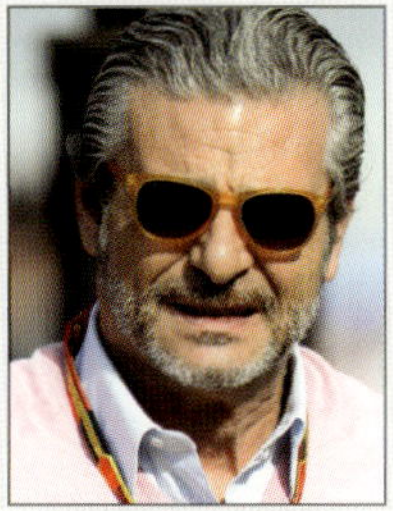

MAURIZIO ARRIVABENE

TIFOSI AT MONZA

"The Ferrari tifosi running under the podium in Monza."

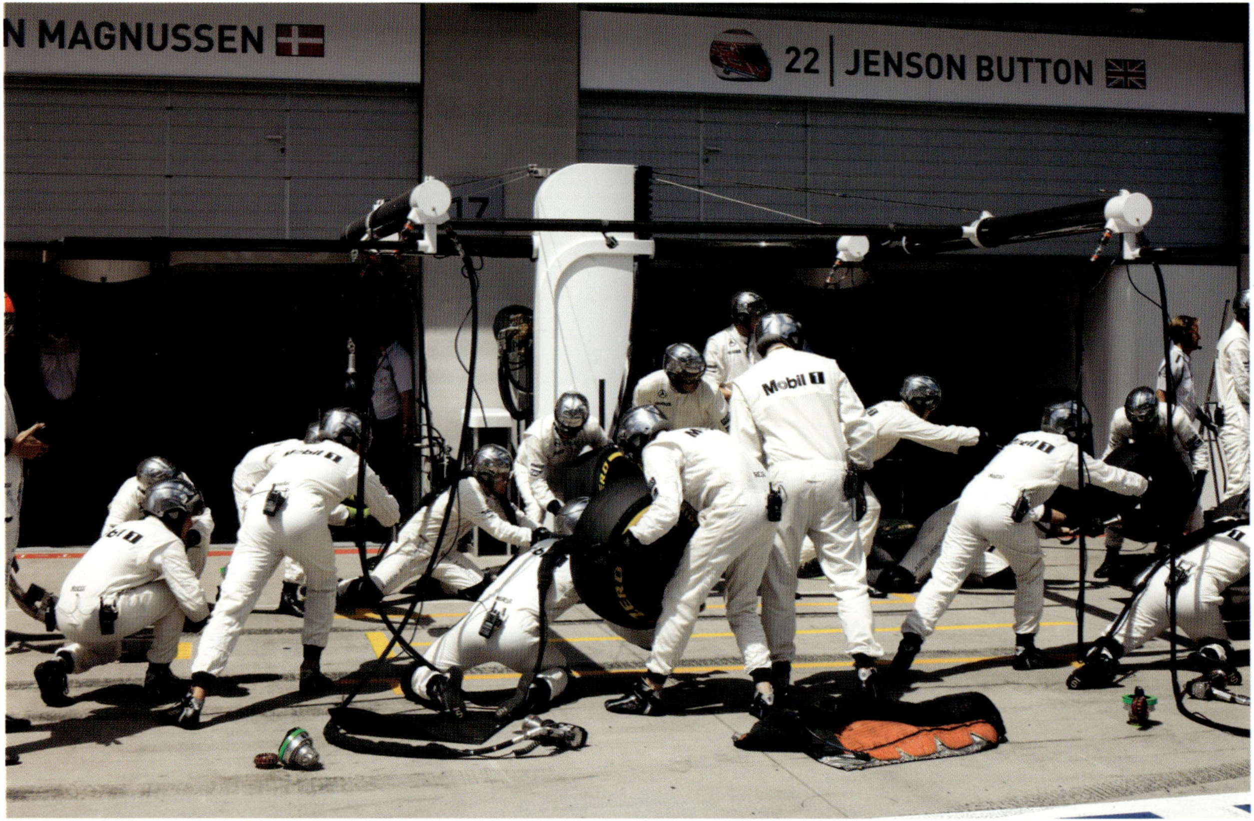
N MAGNUSSEN
22 | JENSON BUTTON
Mobil 1

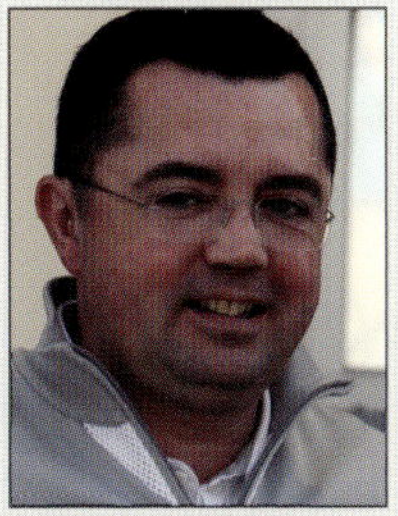

TEAM: MCLAREN

Éric Boullier enjoyed great success as a team boss in junior series before he was appointed as team principal of Lotus in 2010. The team won two victories under his watch between 2012 and 2013 before he moved on to head up McLaren in 2014.

ERIC BOULLIER

PRECISION TIMING

"A view from the pit wall."

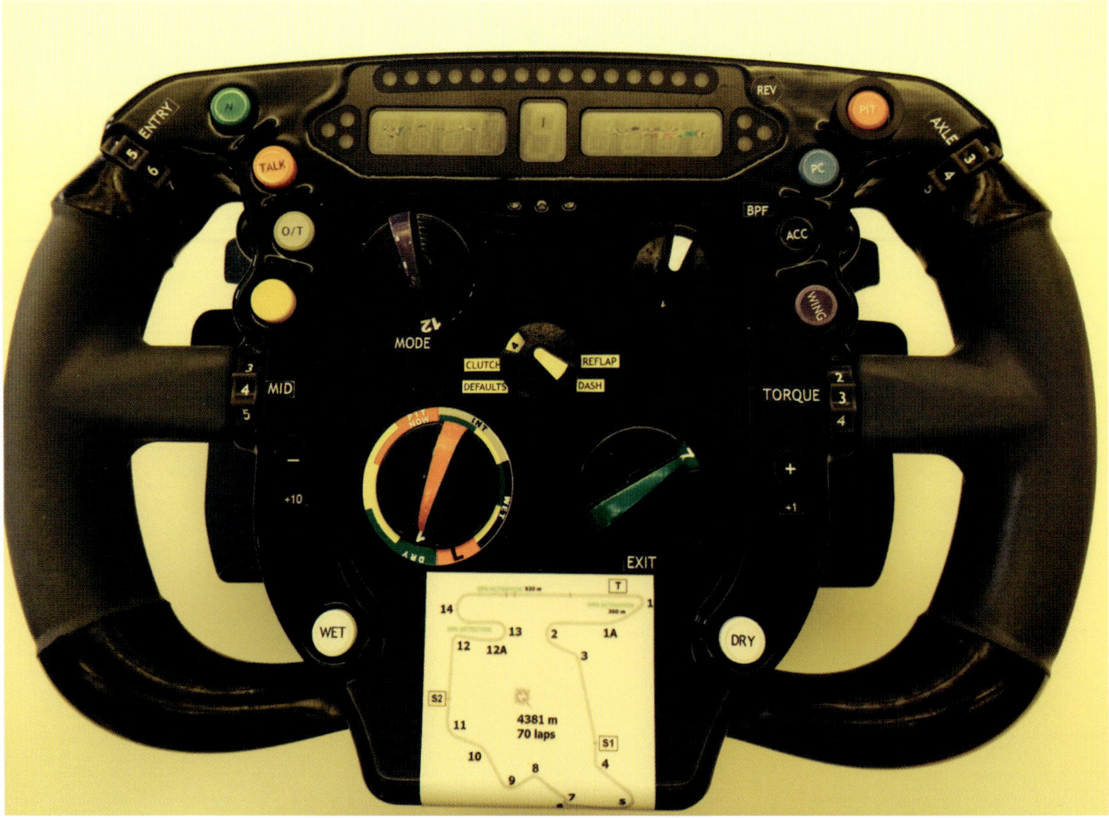
ENTRY
N
TALK
O/T
REV
PIT
AXLE
PC
BPF
ACC
WING
MODE
CLUTCH
REFLAP
DEFAULTS
DASH
MID
TORQUE
PIT NOW
INT
WET
DRY
+10
+1
EXIT
WET
DRY
T
14
13
2
1A
12
12A
3
S2
11
4381 m
70 laps
S1
10
8
4
9
7

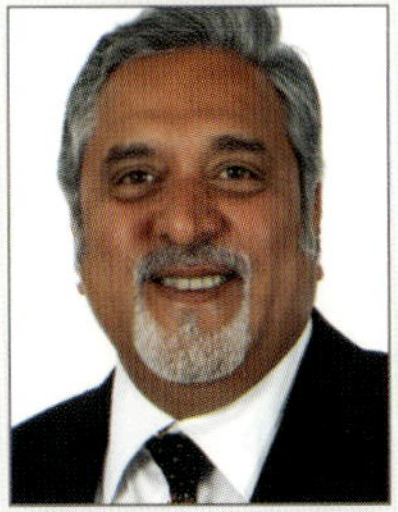

TEAM: FORCE INDIA

Flamboyant Indian billionaire Vijay Mallya has been a fan of motorsport since his childhood and became a F1 team owner in 2007 when he bought Force India. Away from the track, he collects artefacts associated with Indian history, including a Rolls-Royce garbage truck that once belonged to a maharajah.

VIJAY MALLYA

A WORK OF ART

"These days a Formula One steering wheel is one of the most complex parts of the car. With so many buttons, switches and dials, the drivers are kept busy making adjustments to optimise car performance. I took this photo in Budapest to show just how complicated the wheel has become, but also to show its beauty. Made by hand from the lightest materials, it's a work of art and demonstrates perfectly why Formula One is at the pinnacle of automotive technology."

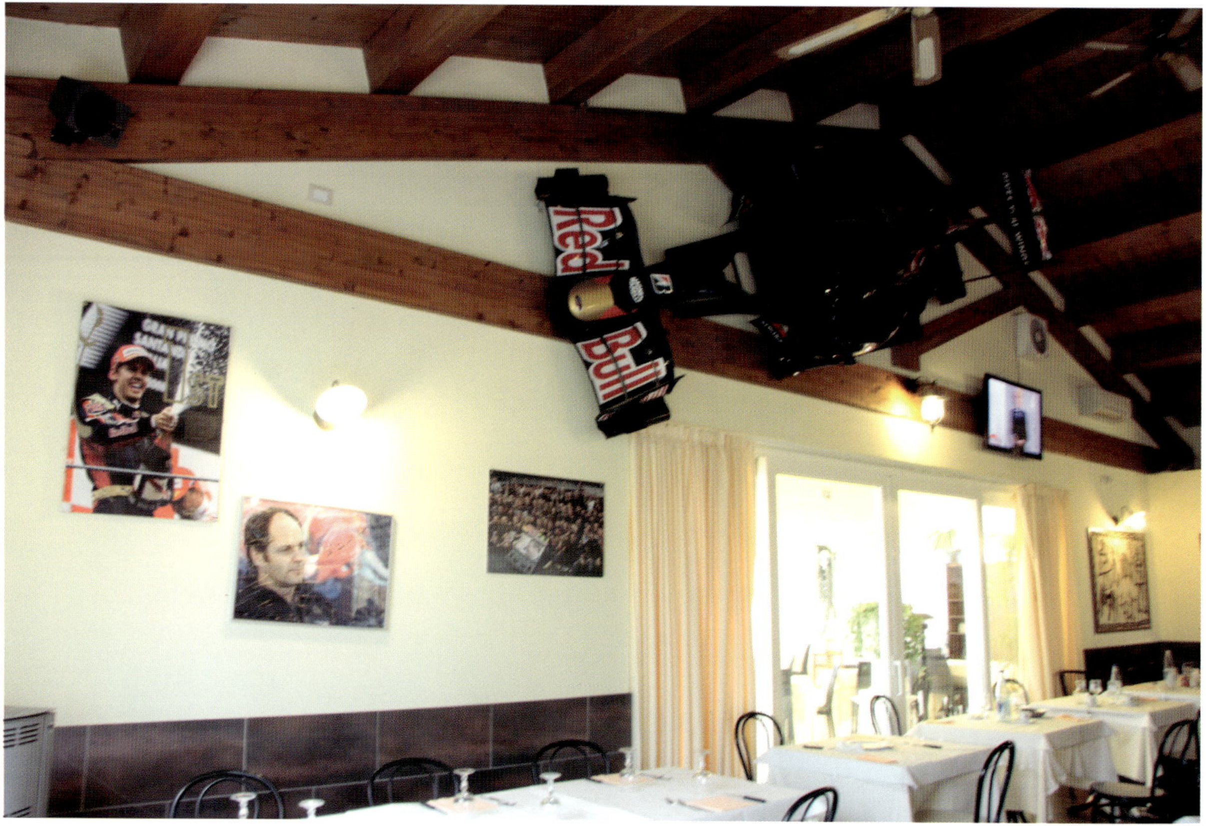
Red Bull

TEAM: TORO ROSSO

Franz Tost got his first taste of F1 working for Ralf Schumacher's management team before he became the operations manager of BMW's F1 programme. When Toro Rosso was launched in 2006 he was appointed team principal and has managed the team since then, inspiring it to victory in the 2008 Italian Grand Prix.

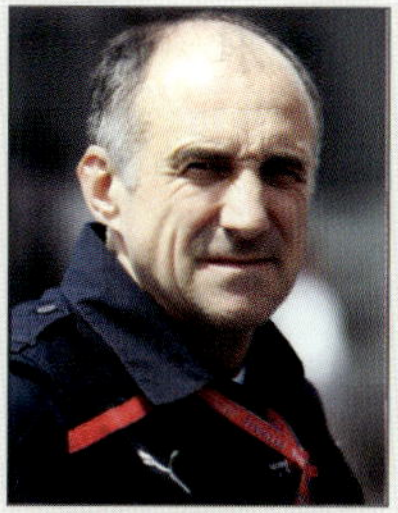

FRANZ TOST

FAST FOOD

"Although we have extended the Faenza factory considerably in recent years, we still don't have a canteen on the premises. That's why, the "Tana Del Lupo" is in some ways the Toro Rosso lunch-stop. The owner 'Zinzo' is a real F1 fan and passionate about our team and nothing is too much trouble for him when it comes to feeding us. He even organises take-away food when the team is working long hours. As you can see, the occasional Toro Rosso car has been turned into "artwork" on the restaurant walls!"

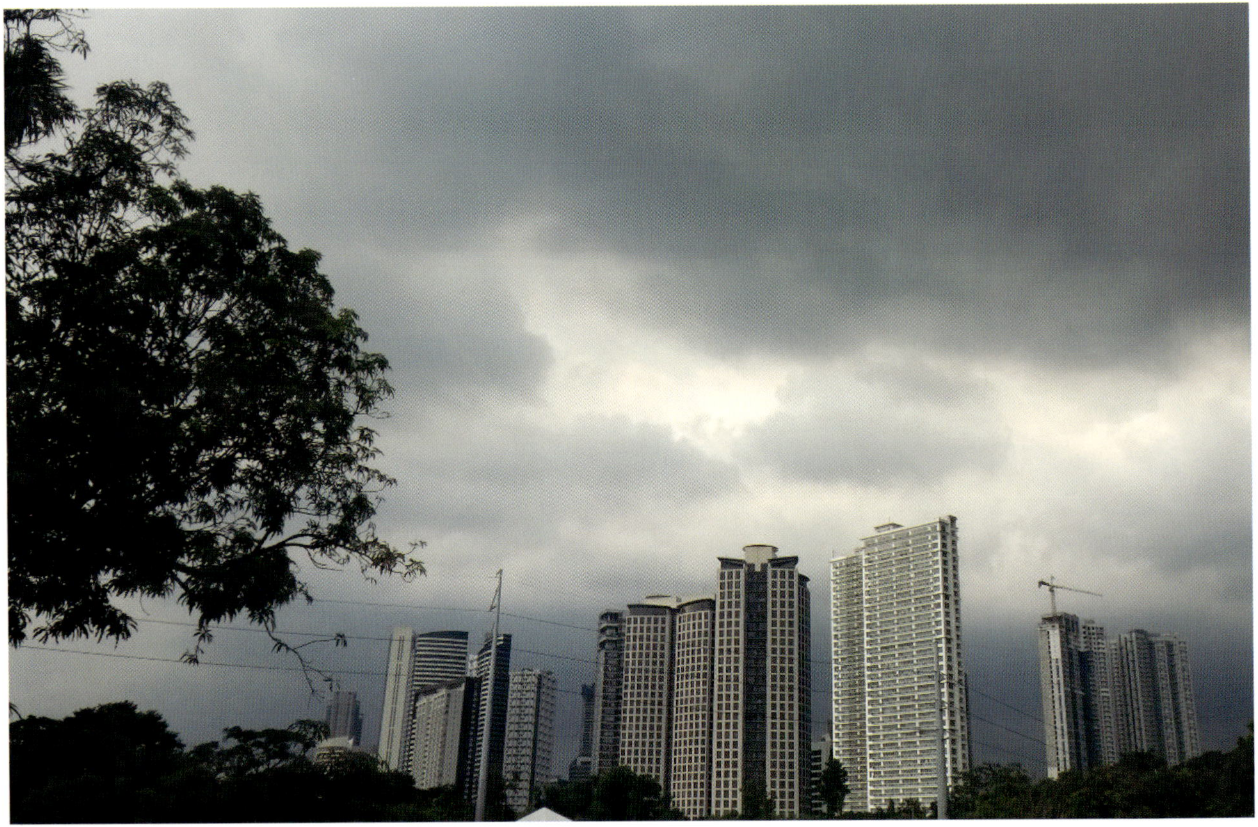

TEAM LOTUS

Argentina's Federico Gastaldi took on a variety of roles in F1 before he was appointed as deputy team principal at Lotus at the start of 2014. His experience includes promotion of the Argentine GP, driver management and working on projects with F1 boss Bernie Ecclestone.

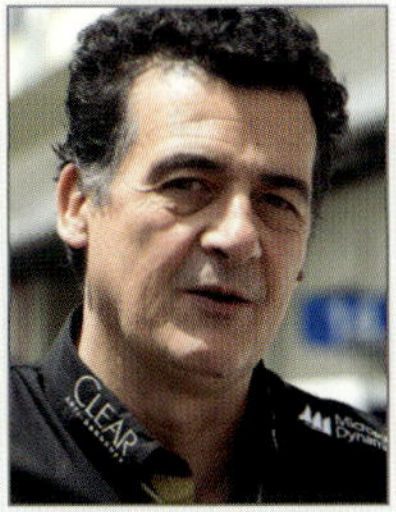

FEDERICO GASTALDI

MANILA SKYLINE

"This is a picture that I took in Manila where I was a few days ago (end of Aug. 2014)."

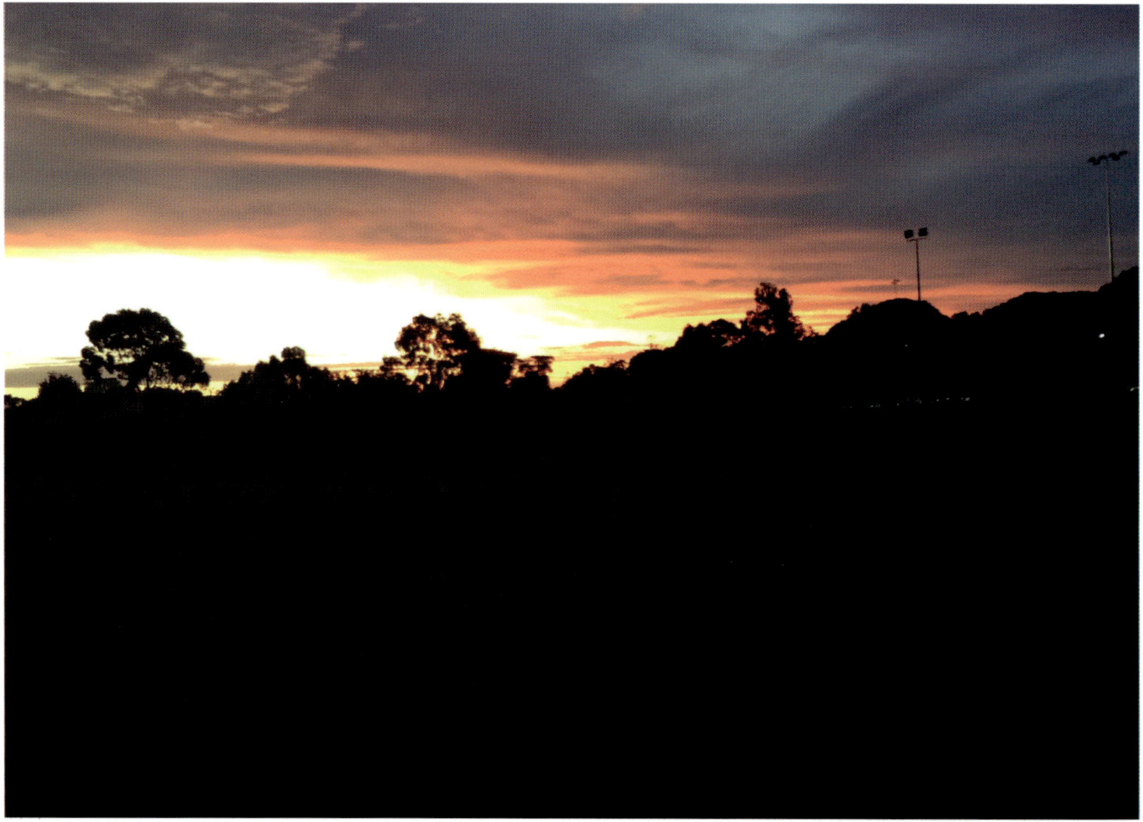

TEAM: MARUSSIA

John Booth set up Manor Motorsport in 1990 and by the end of the decade it had won the prestigious British Formula Three title at its first attempt. Manor launched the careers of stars including Lewis Hamilton and Kimi Räikkönen, winning its own entry into F1 in 2010 as the team that became Marussia.

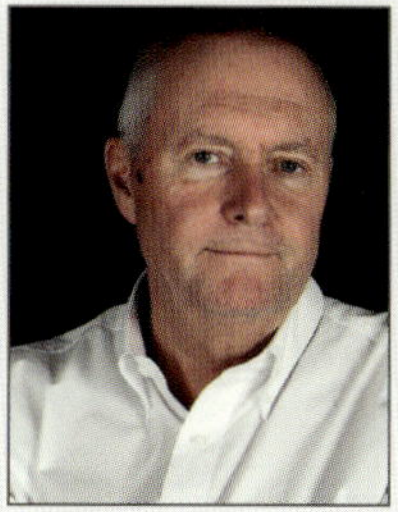

JOHN BOOTH

SUNSET

"A beautiful sunset."

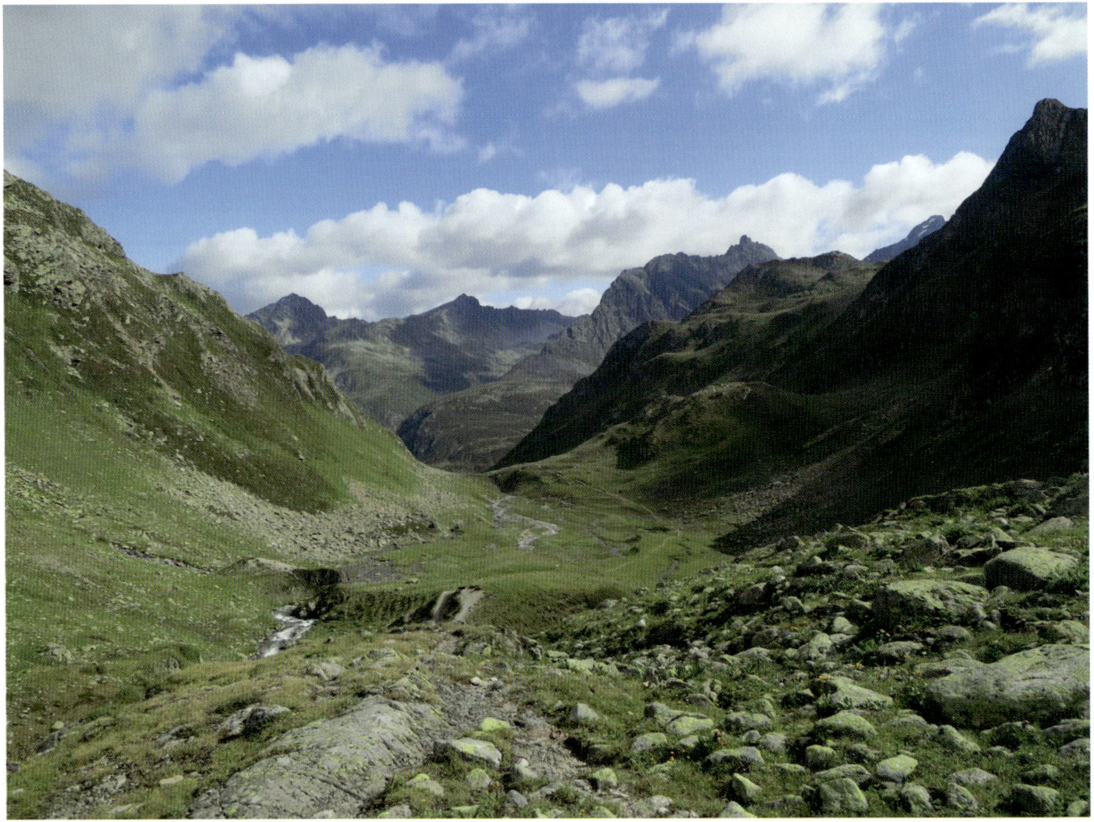

TEAM: SAUBER

As F1's first female team principal, Monisha Kaltenborn occupies a special place in the sport's history. She started out as a lawyer and her first role at Sauber was in this capacity. Following team founder Peter Sauber's retirement in 2012 she became team boss and 33% owner of the Swiss outfit.

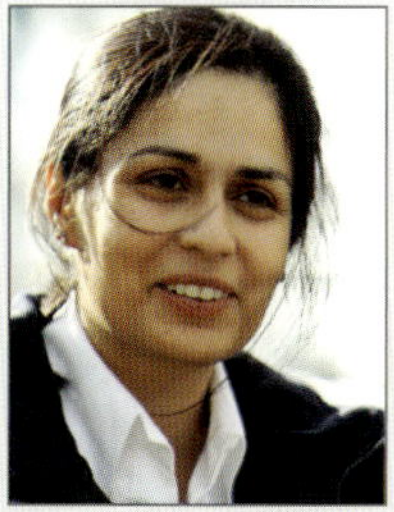

MONISHA KALTENBORN

FAMILY HIKING HOLIDAY

"This picture was taken during a very nice hiking trip close to Davos, Switzerland. I enjoy spending time in the nature together with my husband and my children."

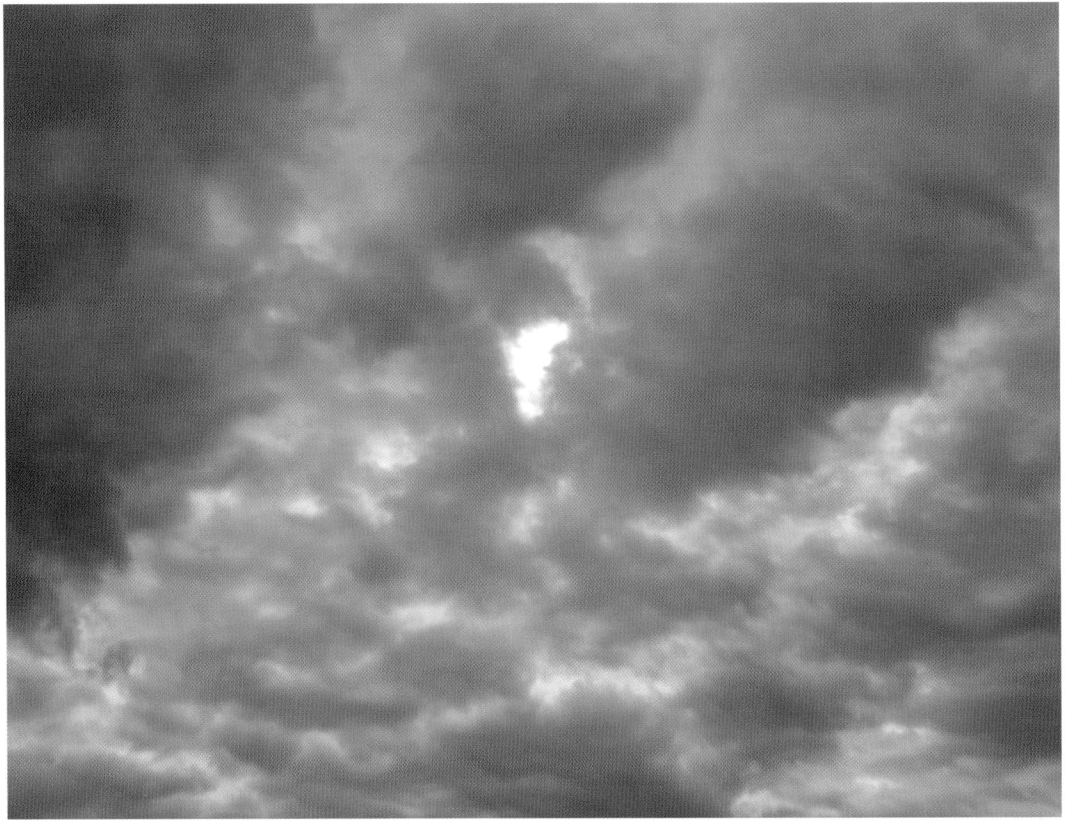

2014 TEAM: CATERHAM

An engineer by trade, Cyril Abiteboul started out in Formula One working for Renault, where he became the head of the Renault Sport F1 engine division. He joined Caterham in late 2012 and was the team's principal until mid 2014 when he rejoined Renault.

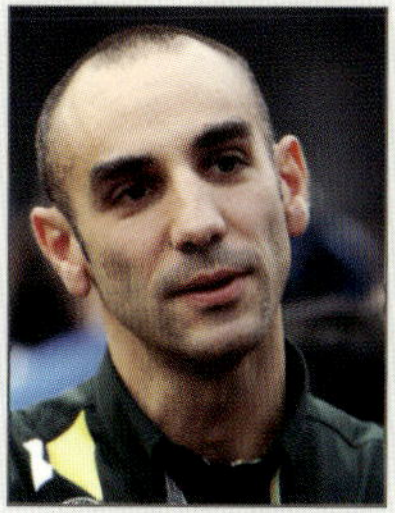

CYRIL ABITEBOUL

SILVER LININGS

"When I look up and see clouds I think this may be our day..."

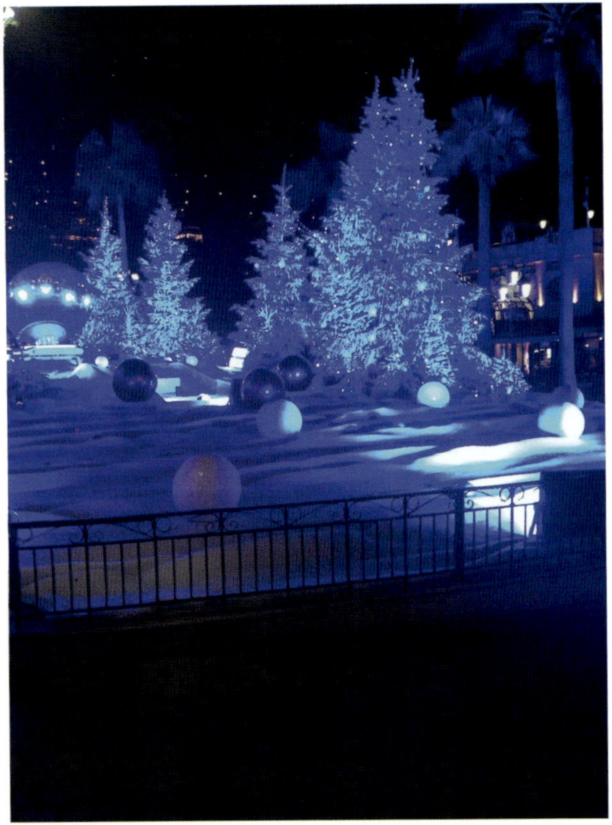

FORMER TEAM BOSS

Flavio Briatore built up a super-team for Benetton in the mid-1990s which placed Michael Schumacher alongside a technical line-up including Ross Brawn and Pat Symonds. It delivered the drivers' title in 1994 and 1995 and the constructors' in 1995 and Briatore also lead the team to a further four titles 2005 and 2006.

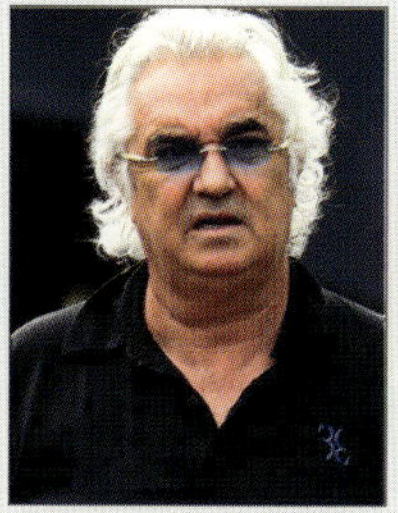

FLAVIO BRIATORE

CHRISTMAS AT CASINO SQUARE

"This is the Christmas decoration of Monte Carlo's Casino Square."

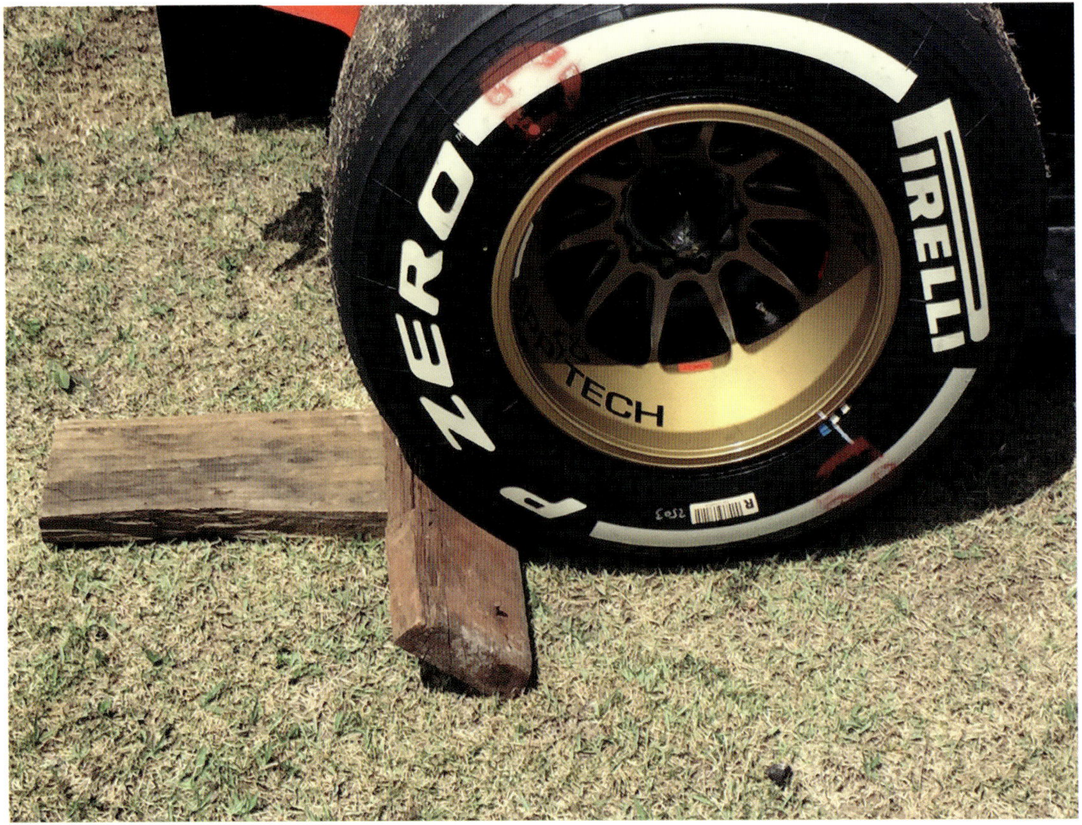
P ZERO
PIRELLI
TECH

FORMER DRIVER AND SKY SPORTS F1 COMMENTATOR

Although mostly recognised nowadays as a TV commentator, Martin Brundle is arguably one of the best F1 drivers never to have won a Grand Prix. During an F1 career that spanned from 1984 to 1996 he finished on the podium nine times and also led Jaguar to victory in the 1990 24 Hours of Le Mans.

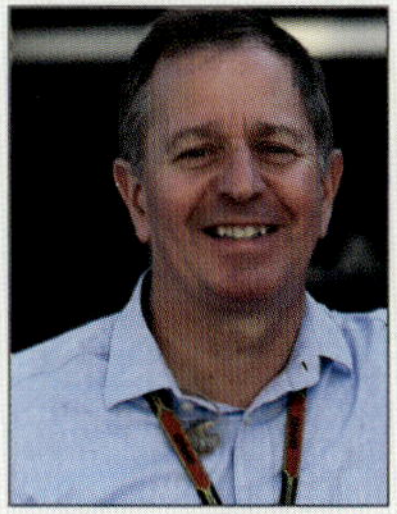

MARTIN BRUNDLE

OLD MEETS NEW

"A low-tech but effective means of stopping a stranded Toro Rosso carbon fibre masterpiece from rolling back onto the track in Interlagos."

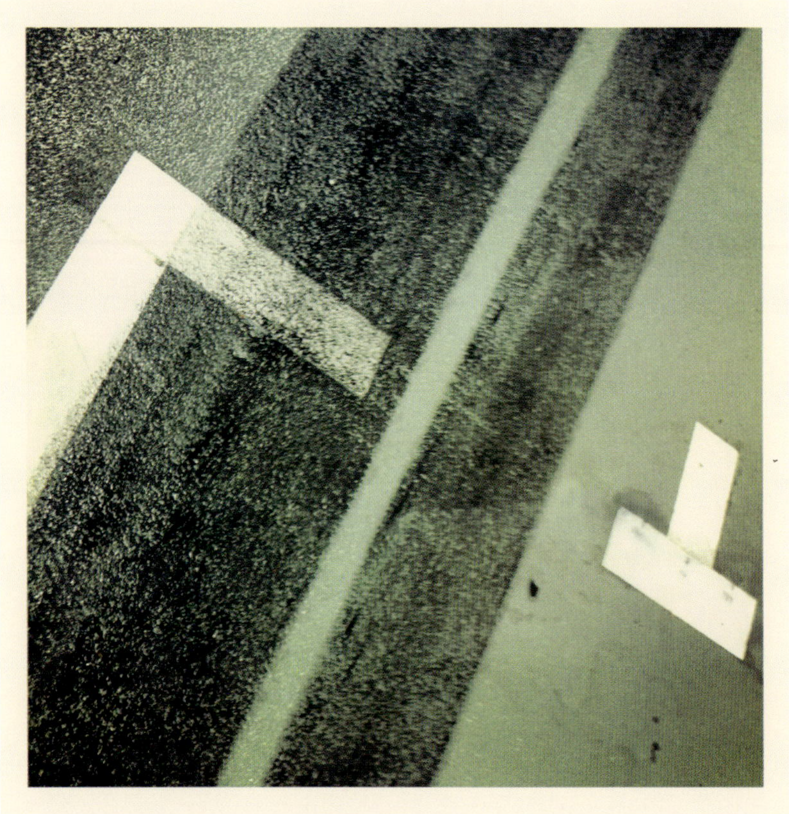

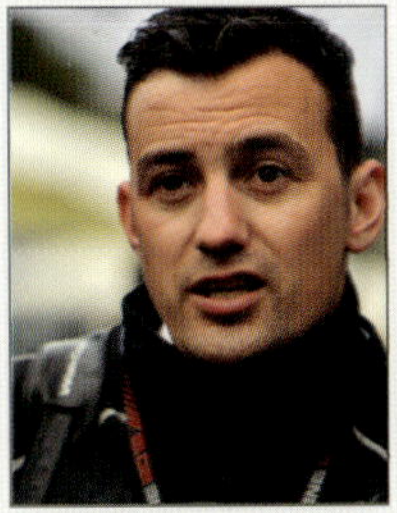

NBC PIT REPORTER

Will Buxton's career began at Bernie Ecclestone's Formula 1 Magazine in the early 2000s and has evolved hugely since then. GP2's Press Officer at its birth, he became the World Feed commentator for it and GP3. In 2010 he became Pit Reporter for the USA's F1 coverage, moving to NBC in 2013.

WILL BUXTON

50 SHADES...

The role of Pit Reporter has changed greatly over the years, but never is it more satisfying than during practice sessions, when we are able to roam the pitlane. It is the most intense period of information gathering for us as broadcasters and journalists, a time where we can spot the design modifications to the cars, watch as the car set-ups are altered, conduct interviews, talk to sources and, perhaps even more importantly, read the body language of those in the garage and the drivers themselves over how positive they really feel their chances are for the weekend ahead. We see so much, but often it's the small details that count.

Under the lights in Singapore, the fresh rubber tracks laid on the immaculately painted pitlane and painstakingly prepared pitbox leapt out at me, and I allowed myself a moment to capture this image at one of our busiest periods of an F1 weekend.

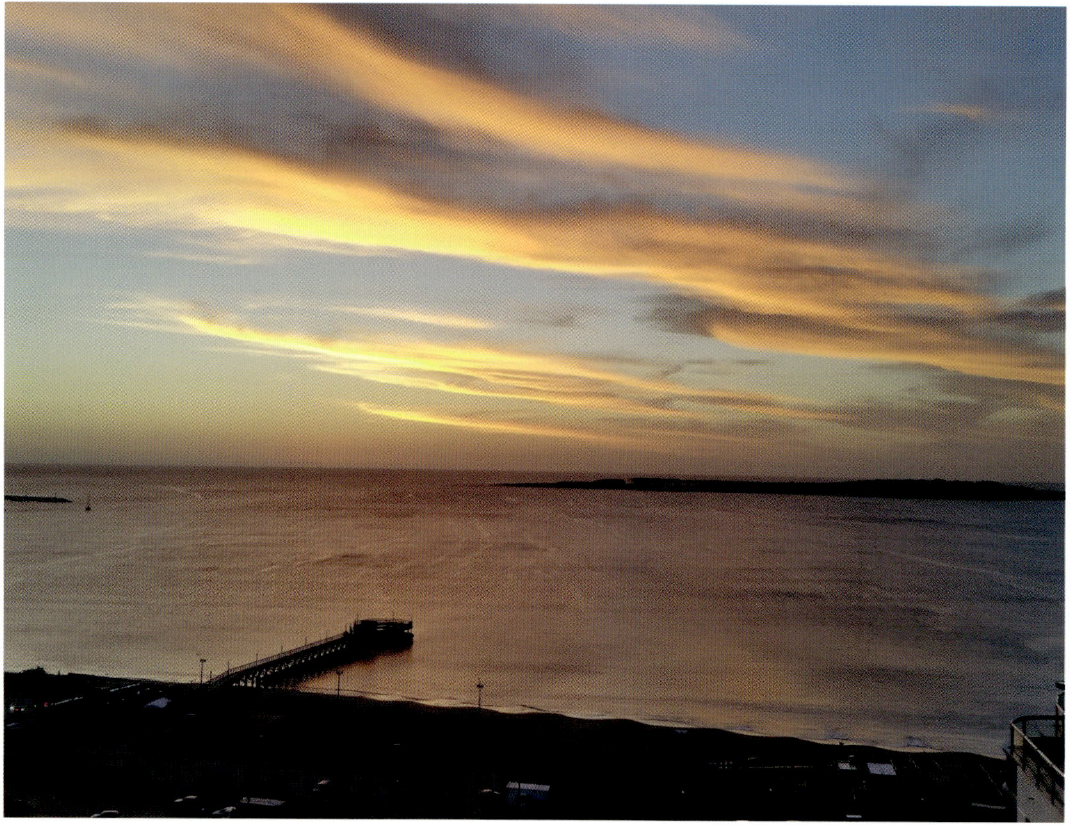

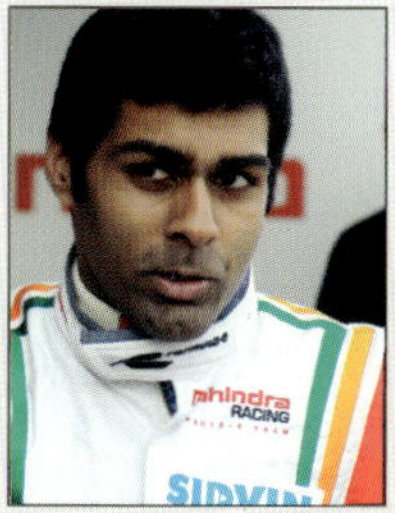

FORMER F1 RACER

Affable Indian Karun Chandhok raced for Lotus and HRT in F1 during the 2010 and 2011 seasons when he was a popular face in the paddock. He now competes in the electric Formula E championship for Mahindra Racing.

KARUN CHANDHOK

WELCOME TO URUGUAY

"I took this from the balcony of my hotel in Punta del Este in Uruguay when I went for the Formula E race. The sunset was really spectacular – it's hard to believe there's no filter on this picture!"

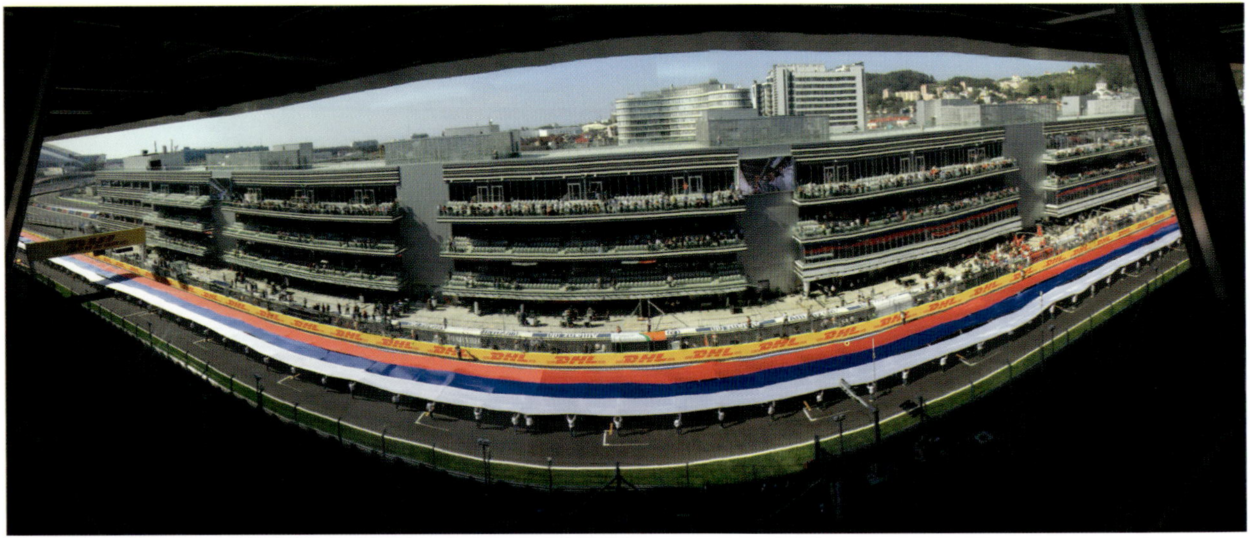
DHL

SKY SPORTS F1 COMMENTATOR

David Croft started out in media as a sports reporter for local radio before he moved to BBC Radio 5 Live to cover events including the World Cup, the Olympics and, in 2006, F1. His skills were recognised by Sky Sports, which appointed him to commentate when it launched its F1 coverage in 2012.

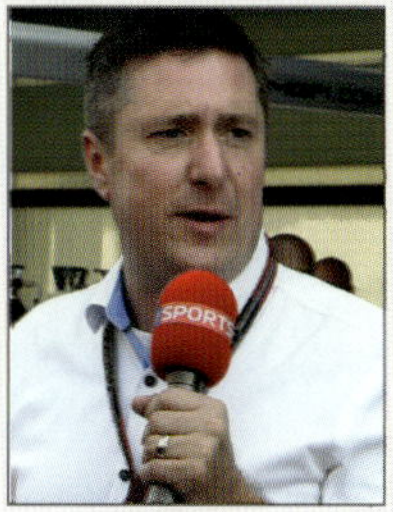

DAVID CROFT

VIEW FROM THE BOX

"Perched high above the main straight, the Sky Sports F1 Commentary Box offered the perfect view of a very colourful opening ceremony for the Russian Grand Prix. So to show my followers on Twitter part of the opening ceremony before the 1st race in Sochi, I took this photo just as the longest Russian Flag I've ever seen, was being unfurled."

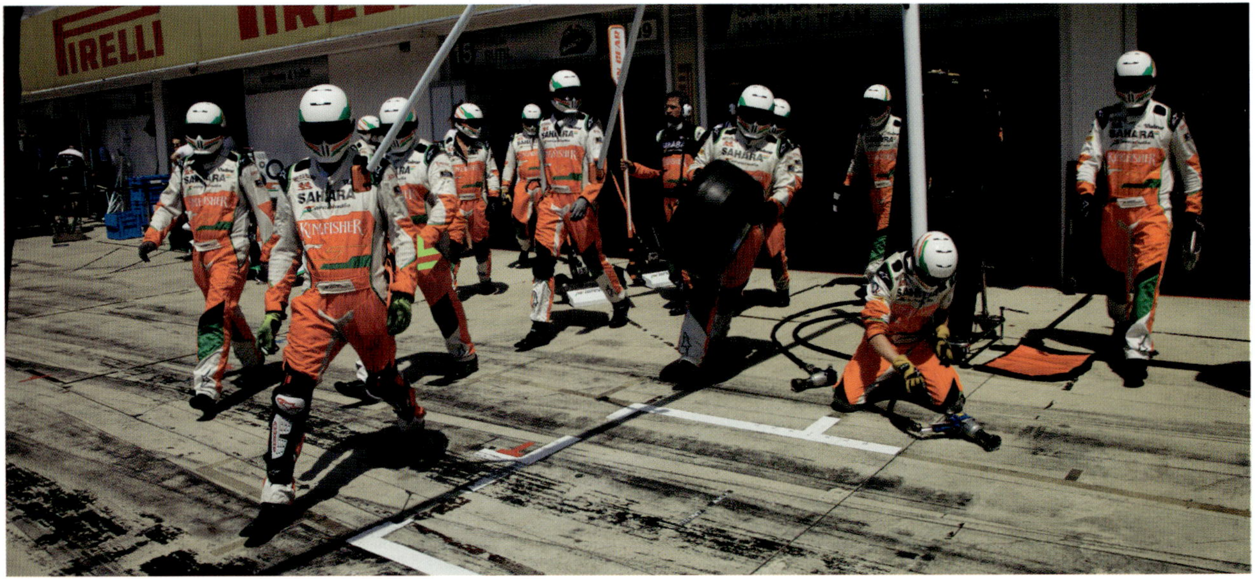
PIRELLI
SAHARA
KINGFISHER

ACTOR AND F1 FAN

Actor Liam Cunningham is a familiar face in the F1 paddock. He is best known for his roles as reformed smuggler Davos Seaworth in TV series Games of Thrones and pilot Mad Dog Maguire in The Mummy: Tomb of the Dragon Emperor and won a BAFTA for his role in crime short, Pitch Black Heist.

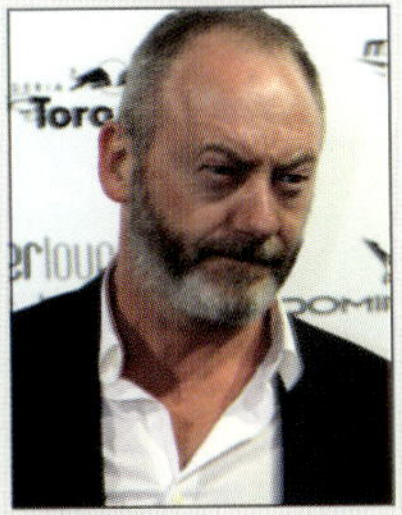

LIAM CUNNINGHAM

A FORCE TO BE RECKONED WITH

"Every time I enter the Formula 1 paddock I get goosebumps. I particularly love the clockwork precision of the pitstops. Box, box, box!!!"

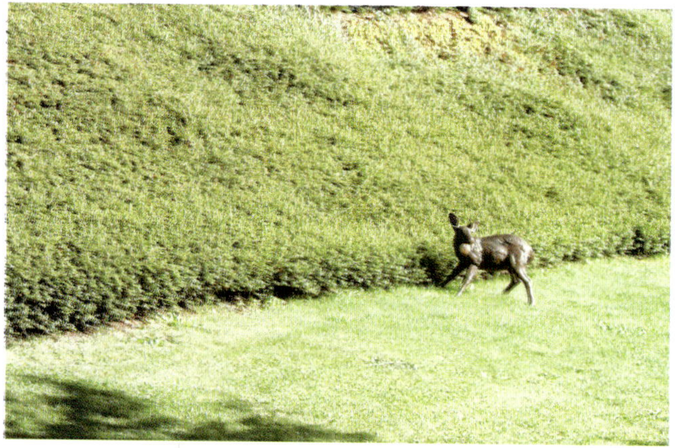

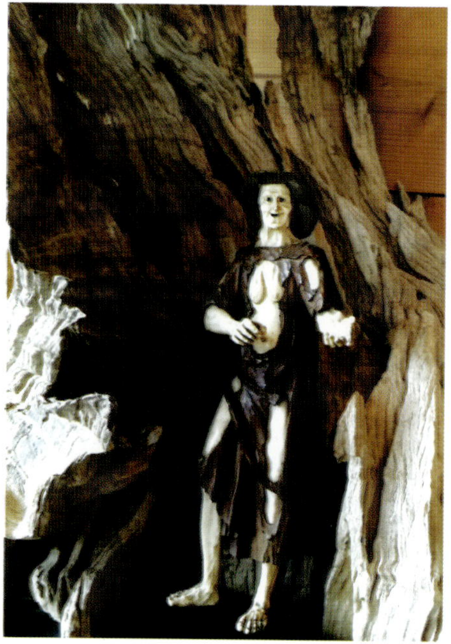

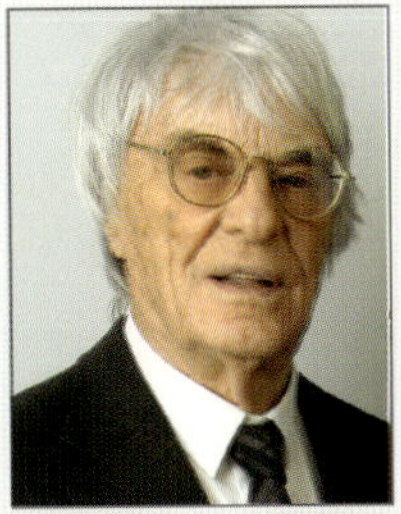

FORMULA 1 CHIEF EXECUTIVE

F1 supremo Bernie Ecclestone was involved in F1 long before the drivers – and many of the team principals – were born. He transformed F1 into a world-class television spectacle and became a billionaire in the process. He is now one of the world's richest men and still at the wheel of the sport he built up.

BERNIE ECCLESTONE

ART AND NATURE

"It's a deer. He's been there for years. He hasn't grown or done anything but there's real deers in the garden as well."

A HELPING HAND

"The guy standing with his hand out. He could be representing one or two of the teams."

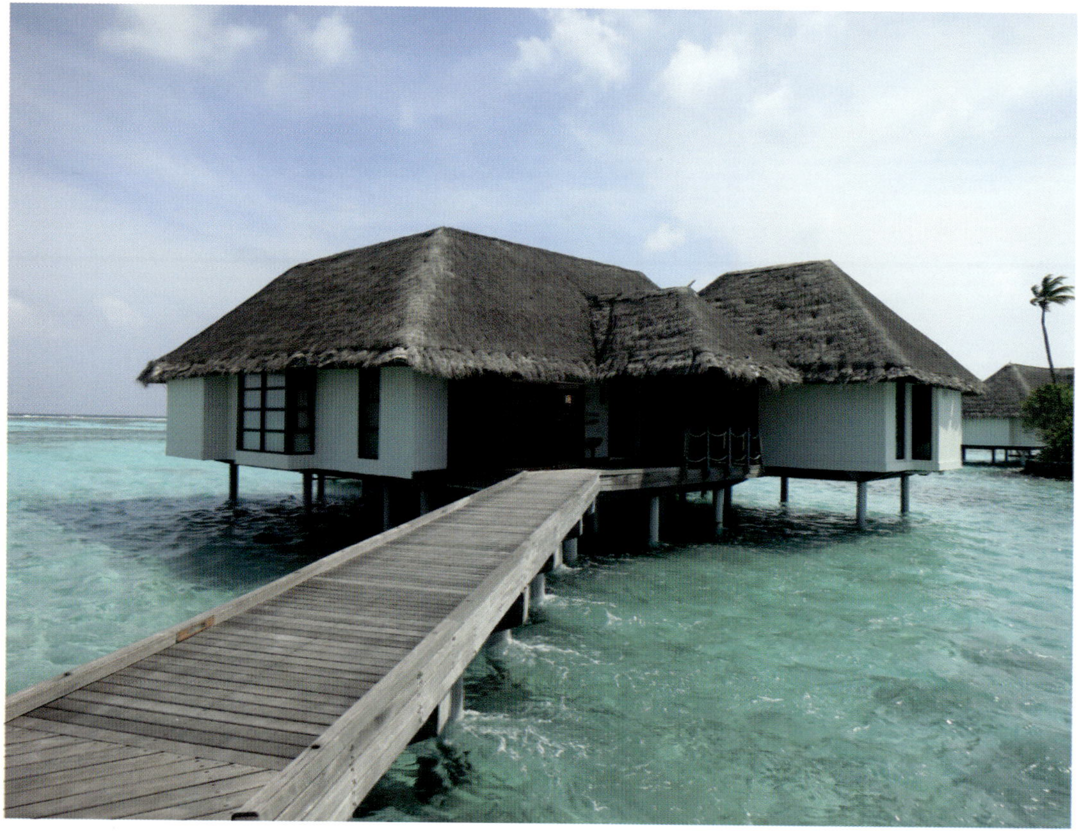

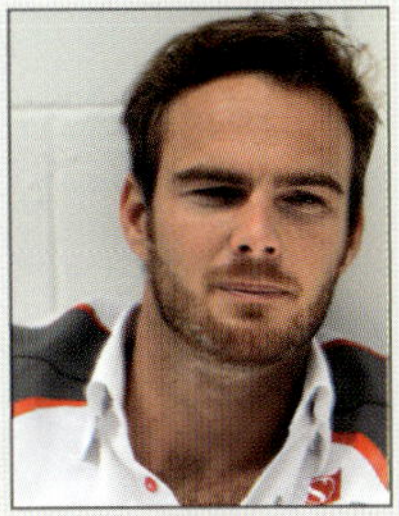

SAUBER RESERVE DRIVER

For a long time it had looked like Giedo van der Garde would never get his chance in F1 as test drives in 2007 and 2008 had both come to nothing, leaving him to spend four seasons in GP2. However, when he took a race victory in the series for the first time in 2012, Caterham gave him an F1 race drive for 2013.

GIEDO VAN DER GARDE

GOOD MEMORIES

"The picture was taken during my honeymoon. After I got married we went to Phuket and the Maledives. This picture is from our house on the Maledives. It was a special place, special location and the first time as married man with some good memories."

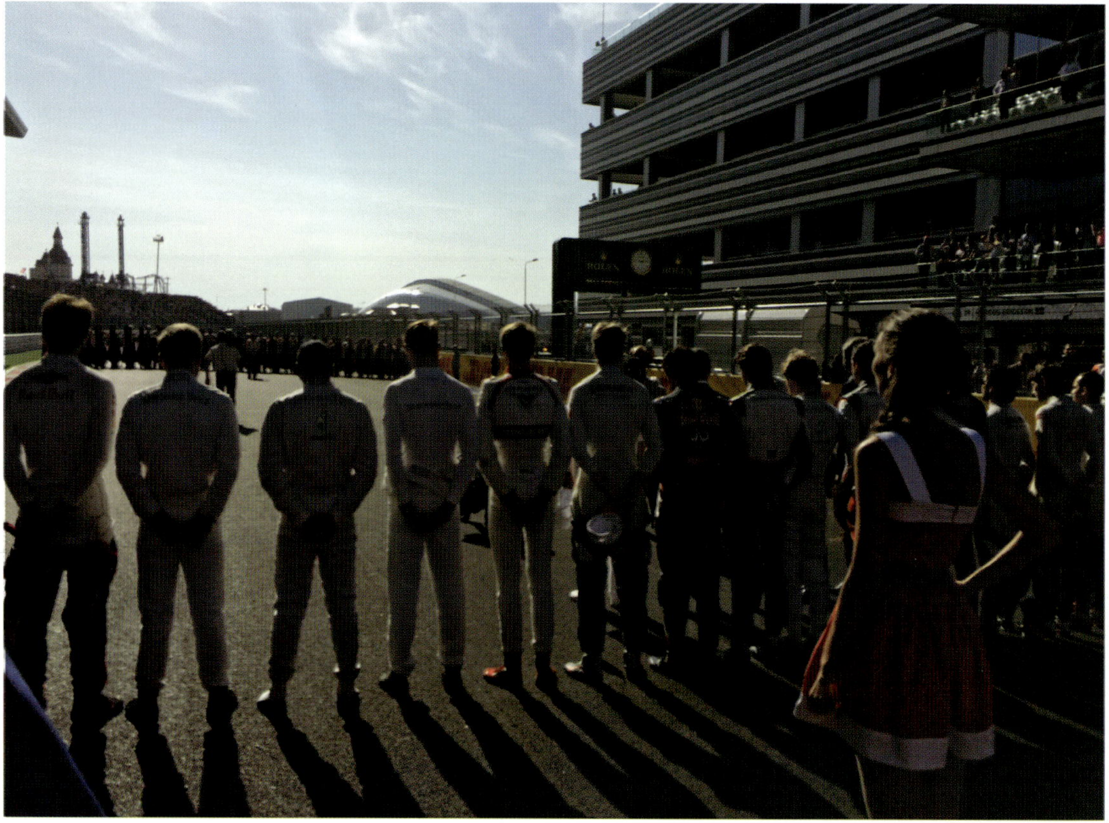

BBC RADIO 5 LIVE PIT REPORTER

BBC Radio 5 Live pit reporter Jennie Gow joined BBC Sport as a production secretary in 1999 and has worked her way up through the ranks since then to become the BBC's F1 pitlane reporter. She is also the presenter of ITV's FIA Formula E Championship coverage and has featured on the BBC's F1 TV broadcasts.

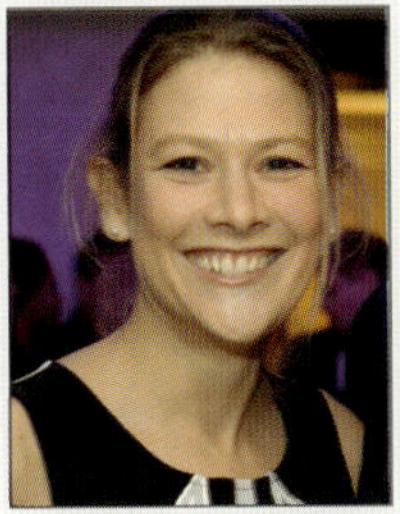

JENNIE GOW

FROM RUSSIA WITH LOVE

"Solidarity: Russia #ForzaJules"

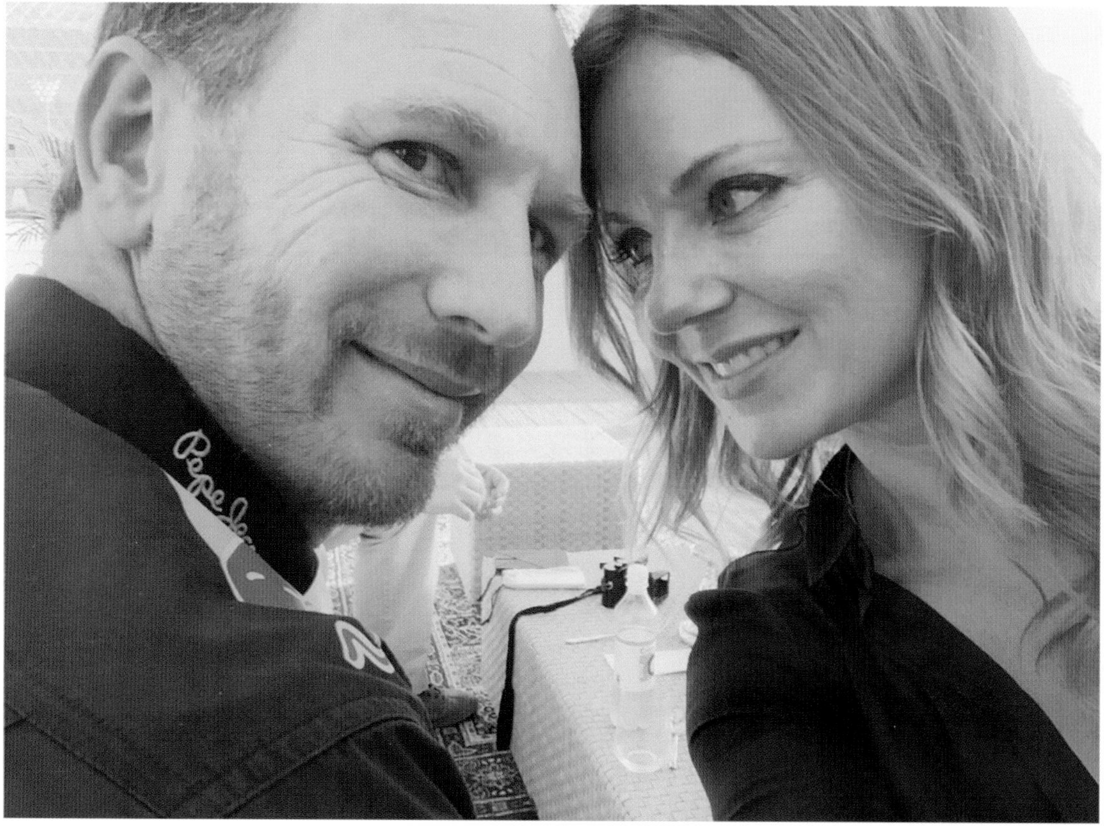

FORMER SPICE GIRL AND F1 FAN

Geri Halliwell is most famous as a member of the Spice Girls, but she is a long-standing fan of F1 and is a regular in the paddock. She has even more of a reason to attend races nowadays as she got engaged to Red Bull Racing boss Christian Horner in November 2014.

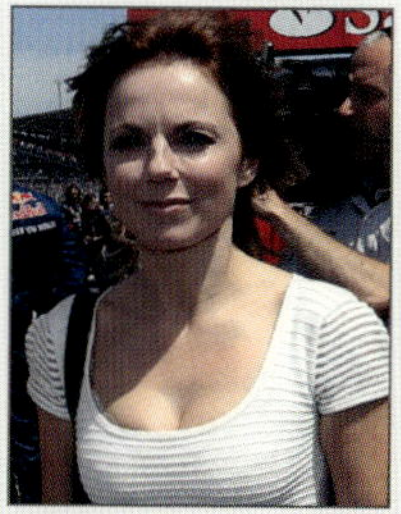

GERI HALLIWELL

ME AND MY MAN

"A selfie with my fiancé, Christian Horner."

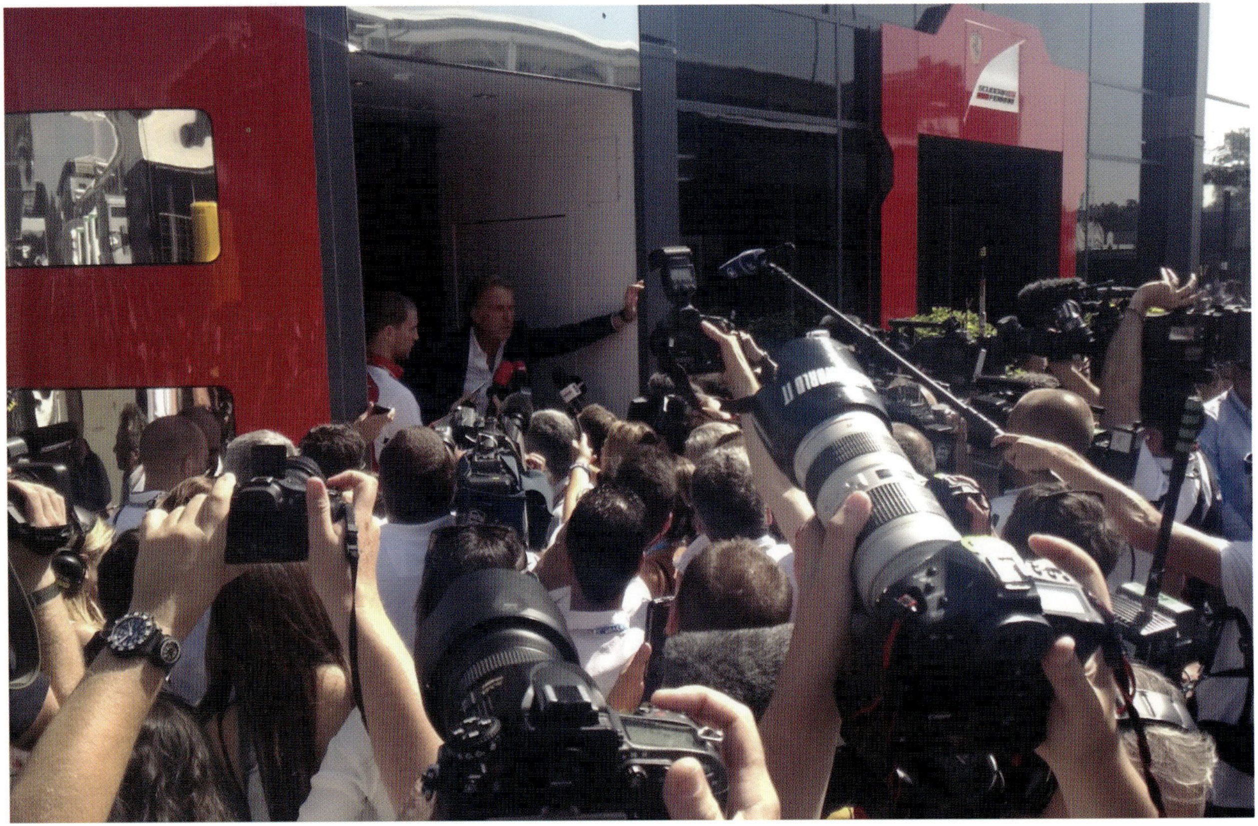

1996 WORLD CHAMPION

Damon Hill is the only son of an F1 world champion to win the world championship himself. Following in his father Graham's footsteps he took a well-earned victory in 1996 after finishing second in the two previous seasons. He is currently one of the presenters on Sky's F1 broadcast.

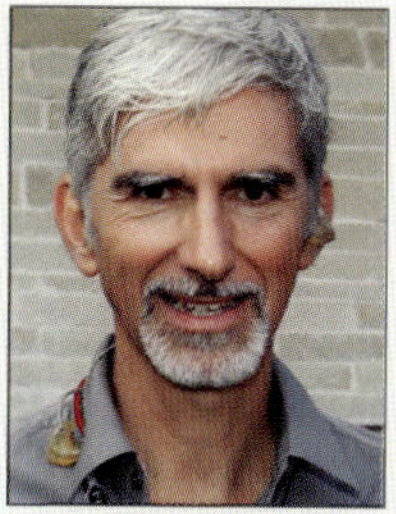

DAMON HILL

"SAY HELLO, WAVE GOODBYE?

I was presenting with SKY in the Monza Paddock when this mob of photographers appeared and surrounded Luca. It was a big show, as they say. He was addressing the masses. Curiously he spotted me in the crowd and waved! I wish I had that photo! Luca must have known this would be his last appearance as head of Ferrari....or he was hoping it wouldn't be. Either way, it was classic Italian political display. Like an Emperor in the Coliseum, or the Forum, like Julius Caesar. Et tu Brutus?"

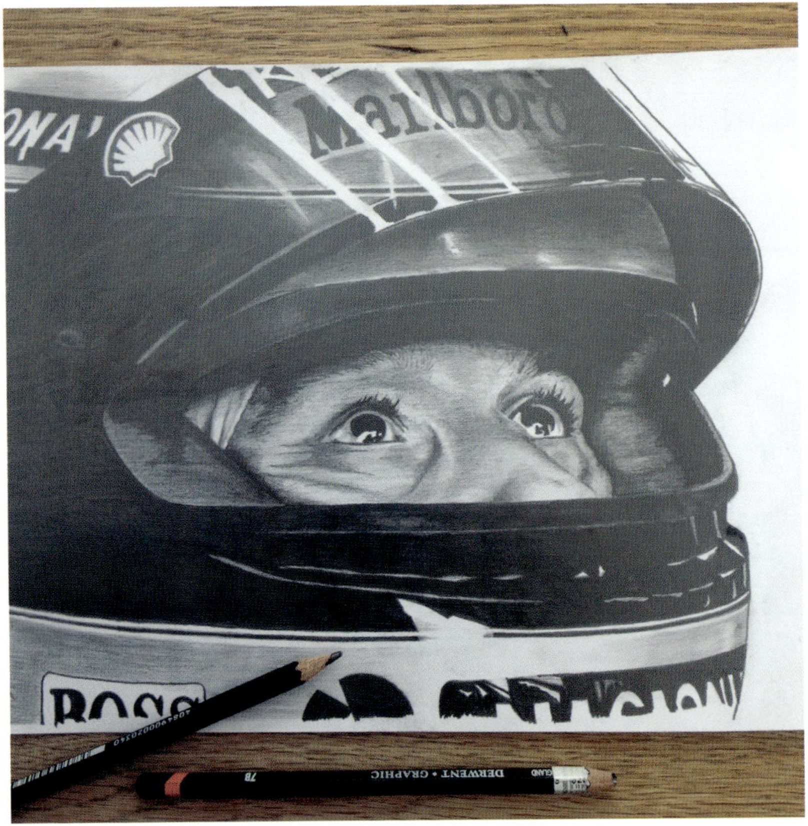
Marlboro
DERWENT • GRAPHIC
7B

MARUSSIA F1 TEAM PRESIDENT

Graeme Lowdon's first taste of motorsport came when he arranged an IndyCar sponsorship for his technology company employer. He subsequently founded a Formula Renault team before taking on a non-executive role at Manor Motorsport in 2000. He was instrumental in the team's move into F1 in 2010.

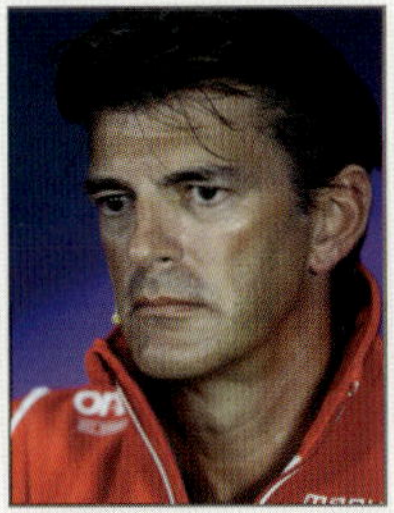

GRAEME LOWDON

SENNA SKETCH

"Everyone knows that Formula 1 involves a lot of travel. This season I decided to spend time on the many long flights sketching to pass the time. I did a series of drawings of racing drivers and this one is of Ayrton Senna from the 1993 season. I was at Donington Park in the rain that year and the opening lap of that Grand Prix was stunning. The flights were sometimes bumpy so it was not always ideal for drawing but I hope that I did the drivers justice."

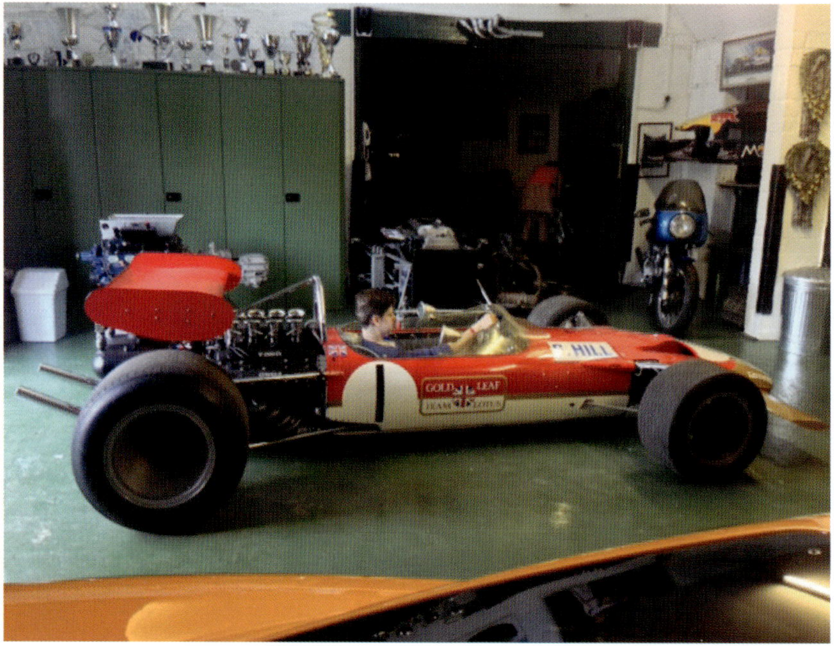
GOLD LEAF
TEAM LOTUS

RED BULL RACING CHIEF TECHNICAL OFFICER

Adrian Newey is widely recognised as one of the greatest designers in the history of F1. His cars powered Williams to five constructors' and four drivers' titles before he moved to McLaren where he won both titles in 1998. At Red Bull Racing he won both titles for four consecutive years between 2010 and 2013.

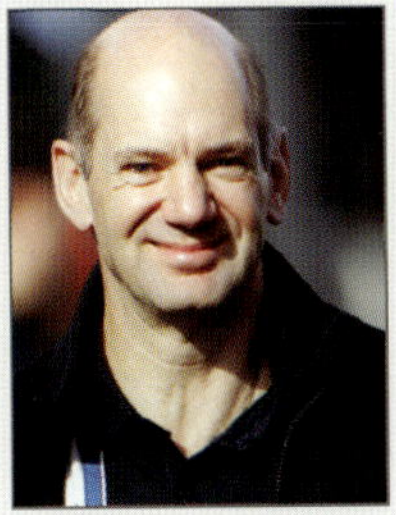

ADRIAN NEWEY

MY GARAGE

"This is my garage at home, where I keep all sorts of things I have collected over the years."

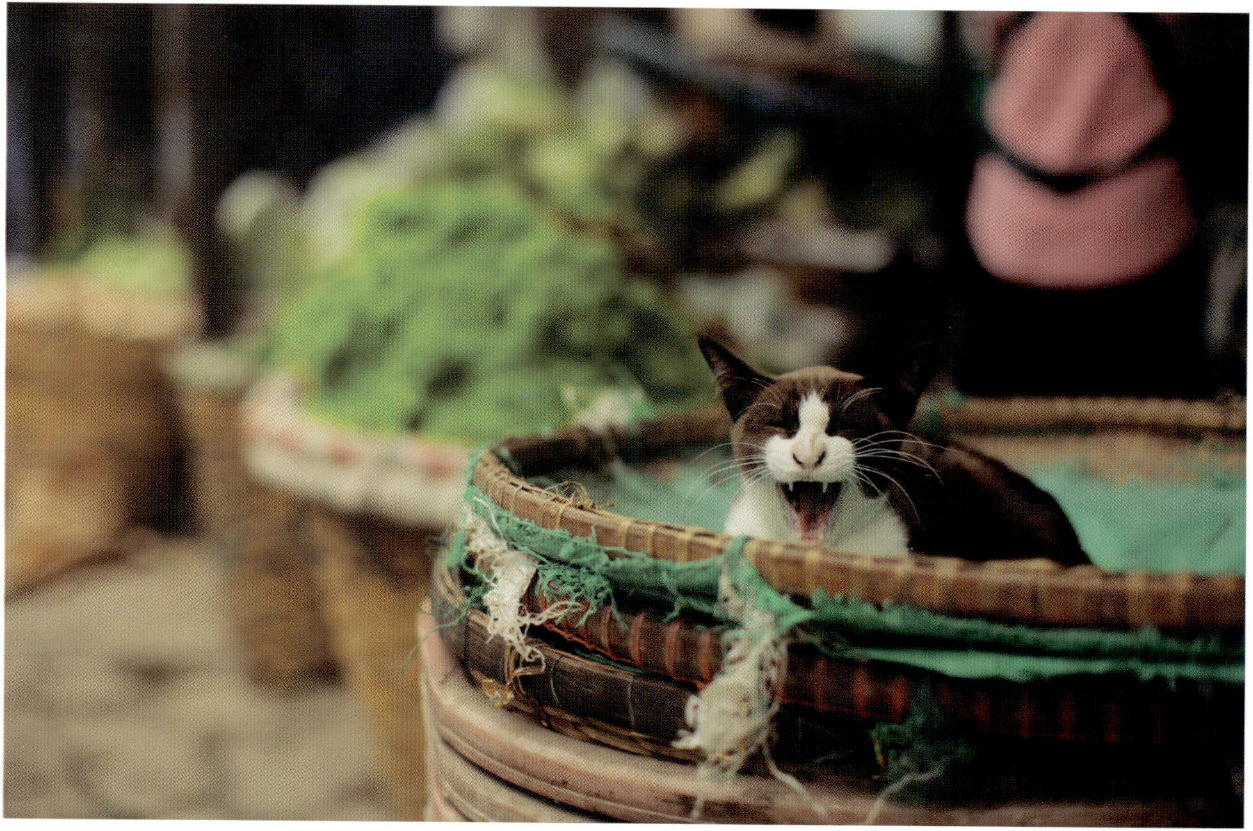

BBC F1 PRESENTER

Although Suzi Perry first presented F1 in early 2013, she was already well-known to motorsport fans due to her 13-year stint on MotoGP coverage. Her cheerful and friendly presenting style makes her a fan favourite with viewers and made her the first woman ever to head-up F1 coverage in the UK full-time.

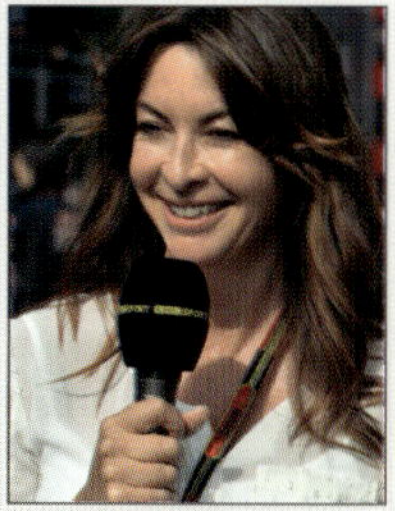

SUZI PERRY

FELINE FAN

"This was taken in KL when were there for the Sepang race. We don't usually get much down time, but this year we had an entire day and night to go and explore. Being a feline fan (aka crazy cat lady) I couldn't resist this little fella. He even switched on a performance for the camera! I would have packed him into my hand luggage if I could..."

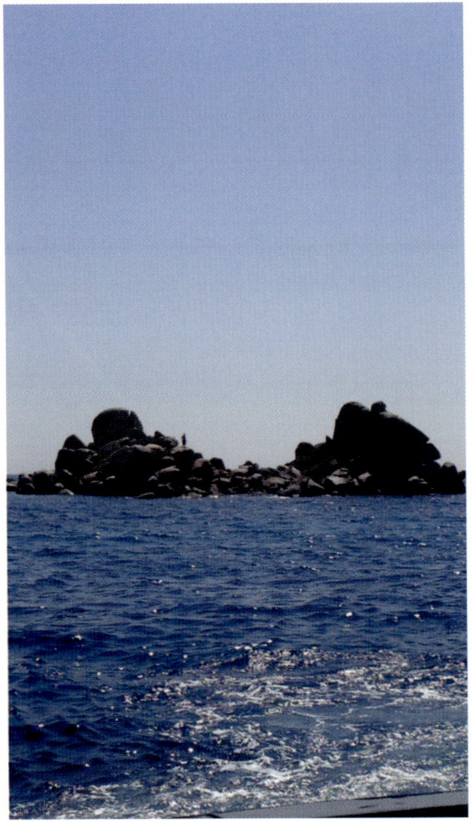

LOTUS RESERVE DRIVER

Charles Pic was exposed to motor racing from an early age as his godfather is former F1 driver Eric Bernard. Marussia signed him to race in F1 in 2012 and he showed his potential at the Belgian Grand Prix when he finished top in a free practice session, a rare feat for one of the smaller teams.

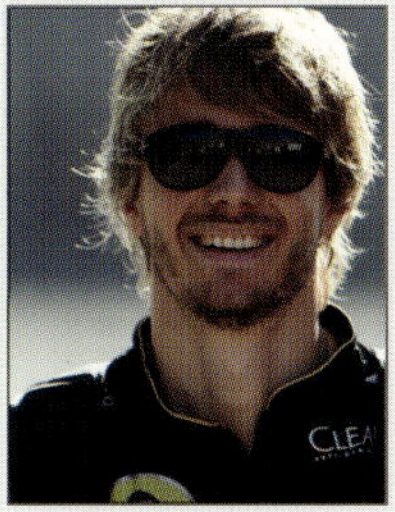

CHARLES PIC

TWO ROCKS

"This is a picture that I took this summer, on holiday, during the F1 summer break."

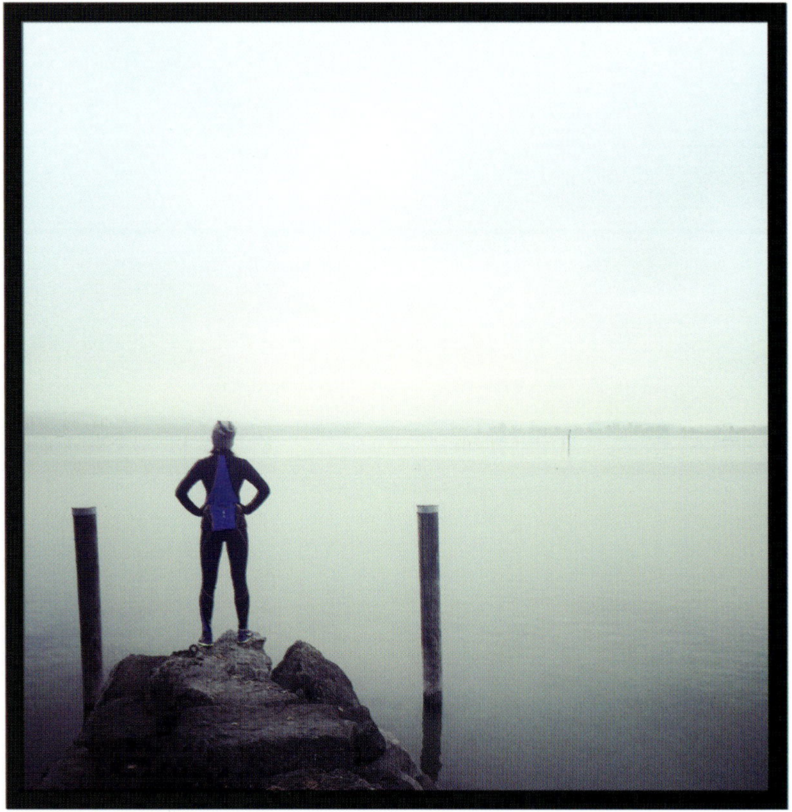

WILLIAMS TEST DRIVER

Williams test driver Susie Wolff became known for competing in the DTM German touring car series where she raced between 2006 and 2012 before she became Williams' development driver. He performance has impressed the team and for 2015 she has been promoted to test driver.

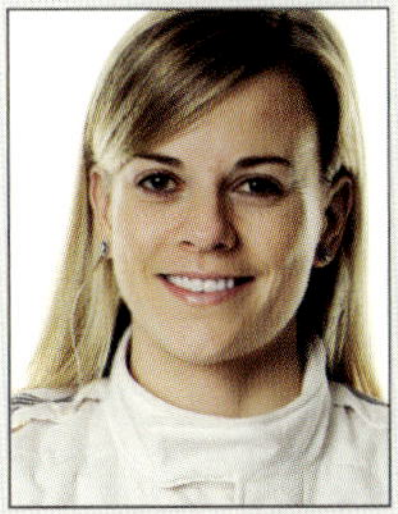

SUSIE WOLFF

LAKE BODENSEE

"I set this on a timer. It's me looking out onto Lake Bodensee in Switzerland after an early morning run."

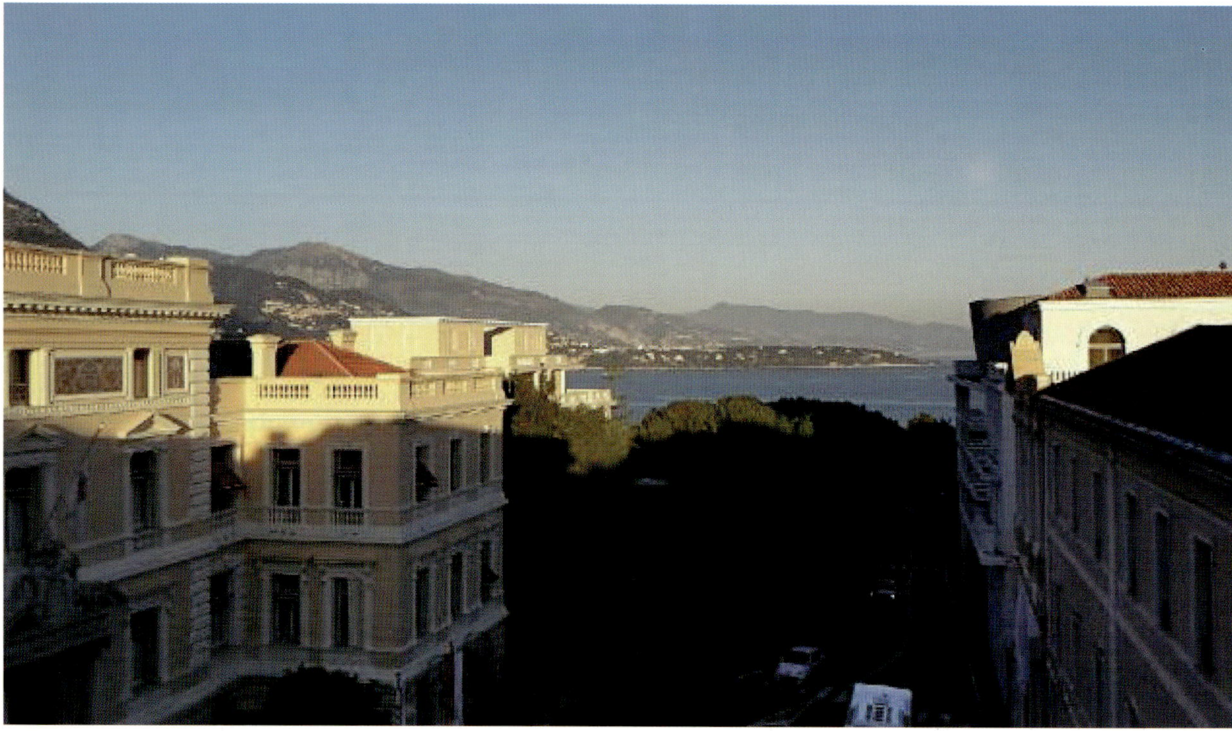

MONACO GRAND PRIX HOST

As heir to the throne of Monaco, Prince Albert grew up surrounded by F1. He got to know the leading drivers at an early age as his parents, Prince Ranier and Grace Kelly, would invite the Monaco GP victor for dinner following the race. He says F1 makes Monaco "a very special place."

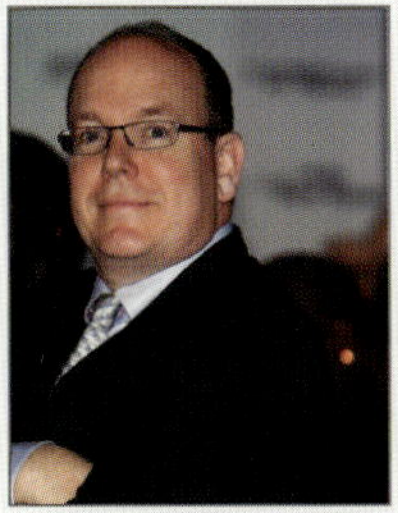

PRINCE ALBERT II OF MONACO

QUITE A VIEW

"It is some view from Monaco Ville!"

ZOOM CARTOONS

We asked two motorsport cartoonists to draw their impressions of Zoom. Here are the results.

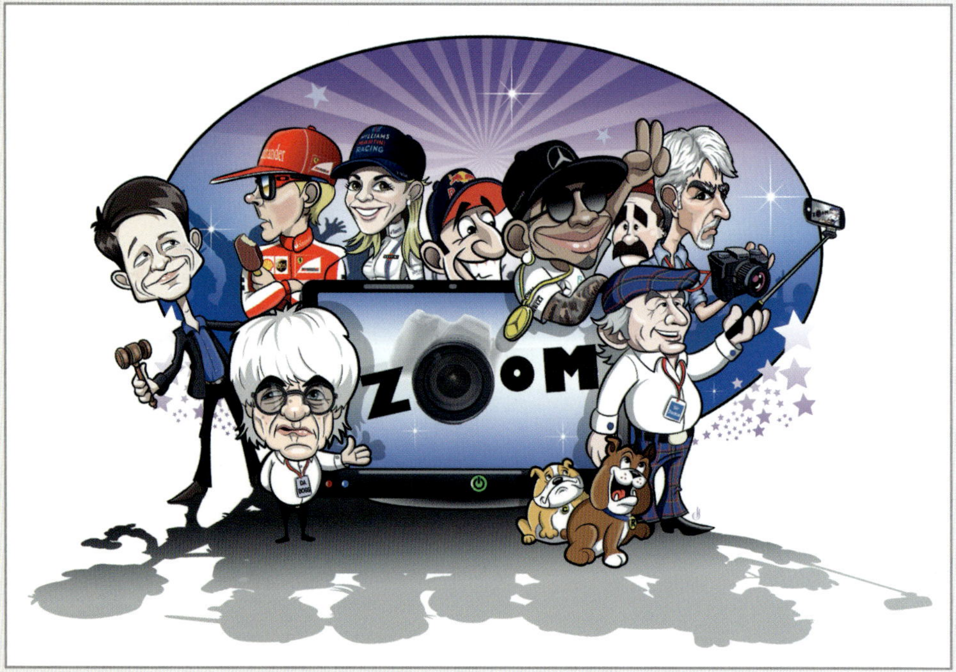

Jake Davis
jakedaviscreative.com

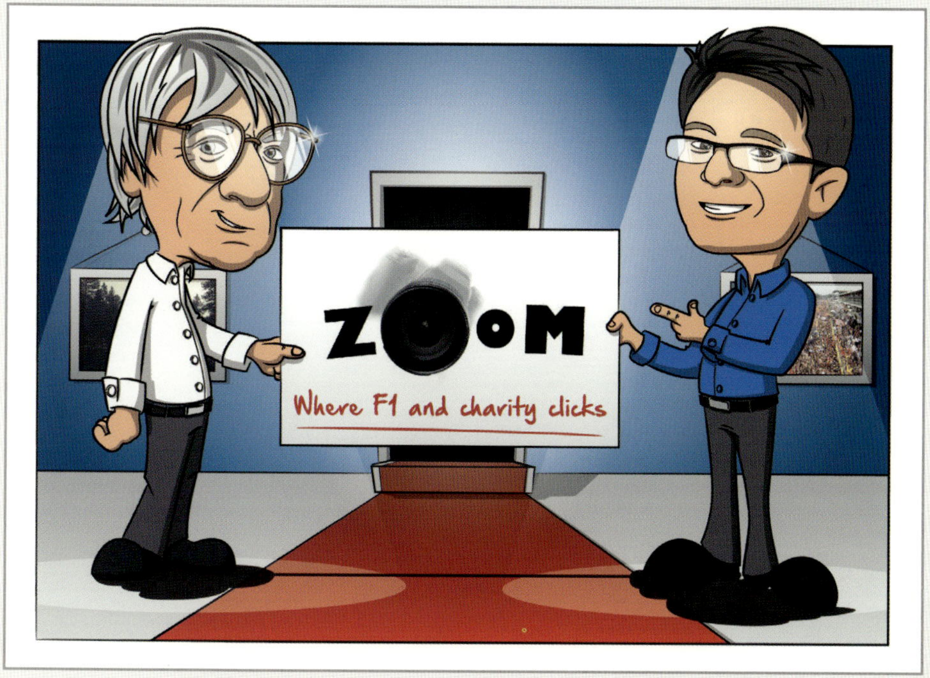

Chris Rathbone
rathbonecreative.com

EVENT PHOTOS

Images from our gala event, 16th January 2015

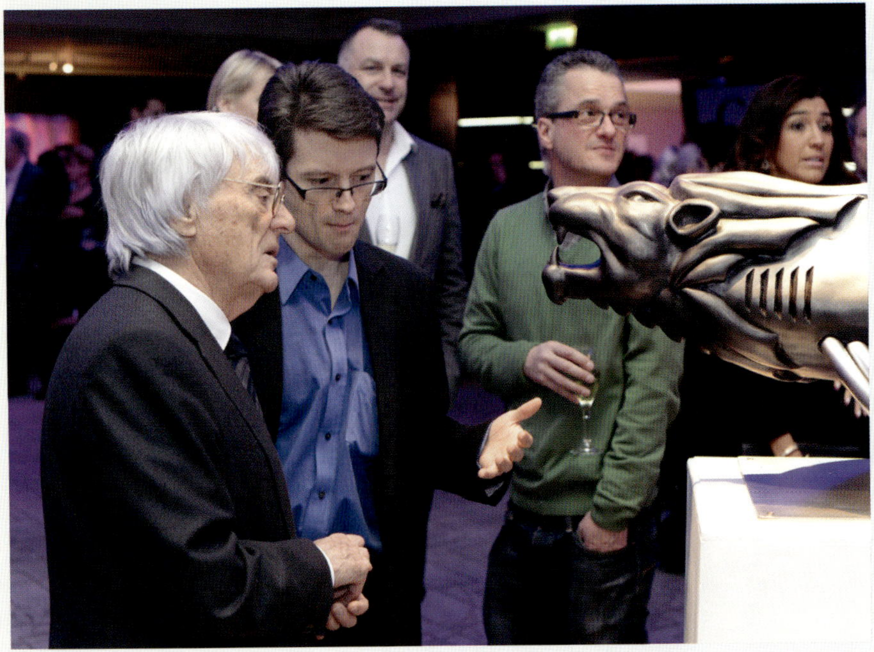

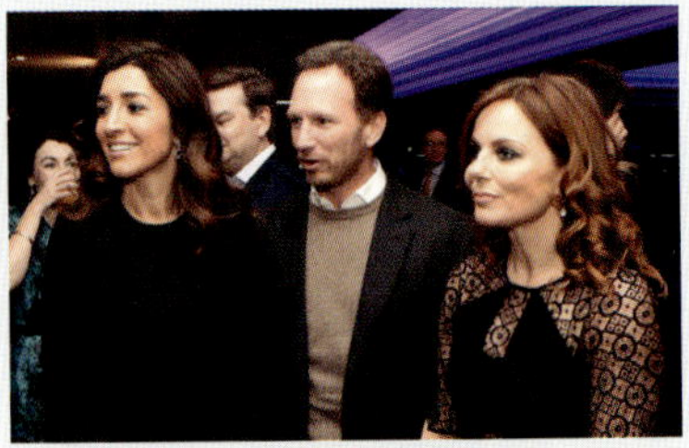

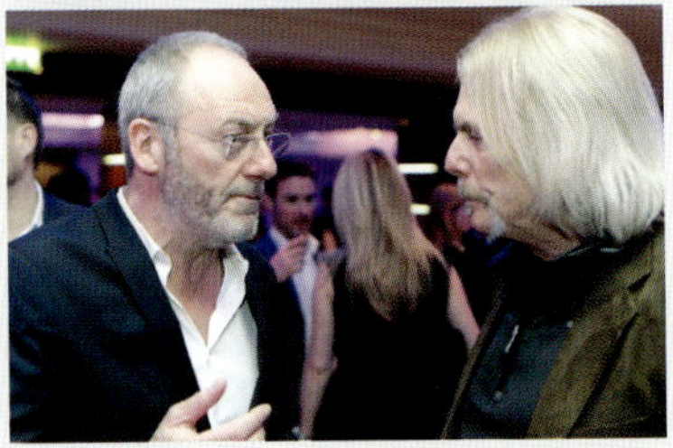

Clockwise from left: Bernie Ecclestone & Christian Sylt; Fabiana Ecclestone, Christian Horner & Geri Halliwell; Liam Cunningham & Scott Gorham.

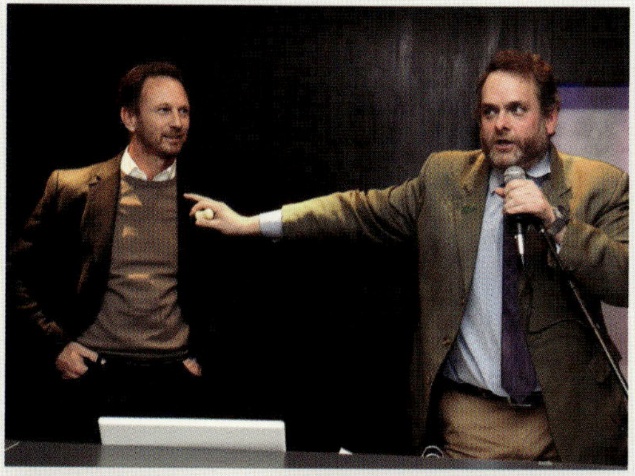

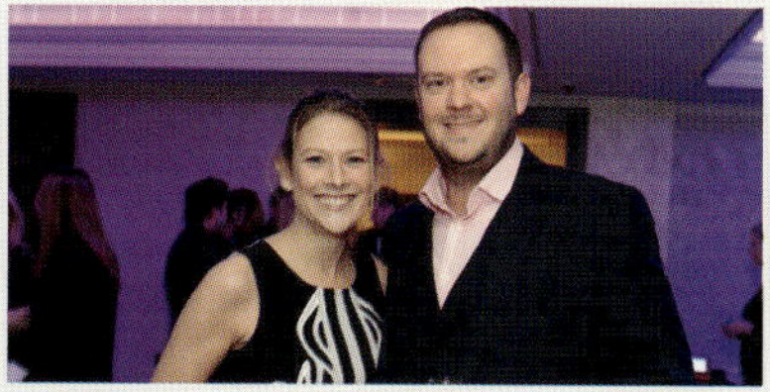

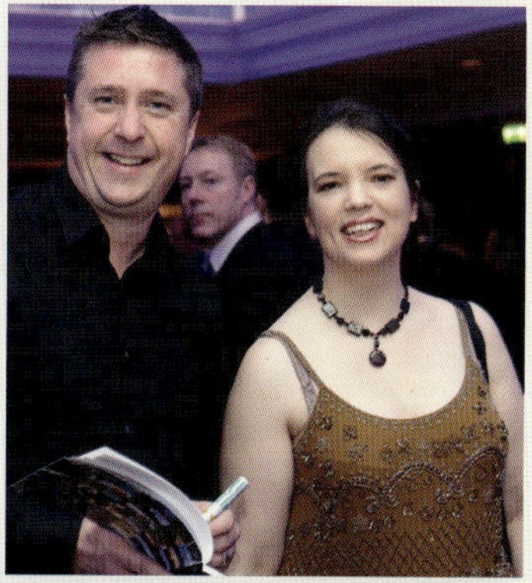

Clockwise from top left: Christian Horner & Chris Routledge; Jennie Gow & Jamie Coley; David Croft & Caroline Reid; Max Mosley, Bernie Ecclestone & Christian Sylt; Amanda Smerczak, Anthony Hamilton & Fabiana Ecclestone.

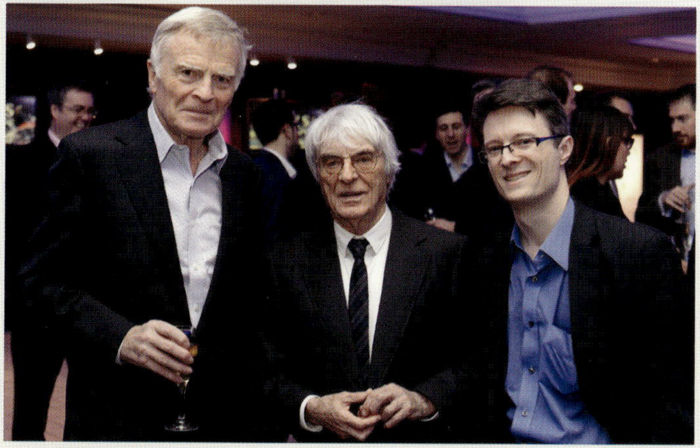

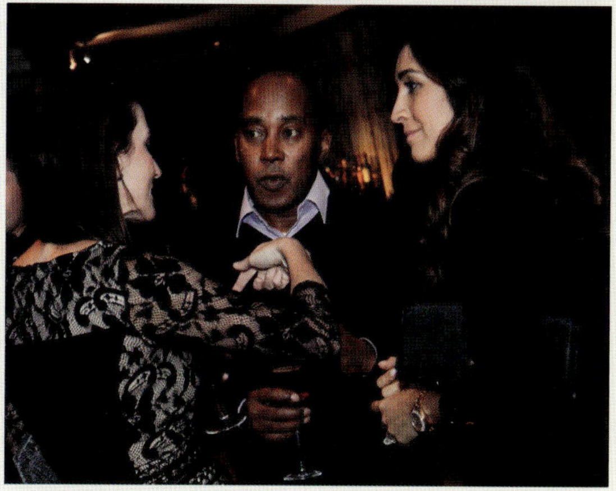

Event photographs supplied by Patrik Lundin, Sutton Motorsport Images and Getty Images.

ZOOM BOOK SIGNING

The stars of F1® sign the Zoom book.

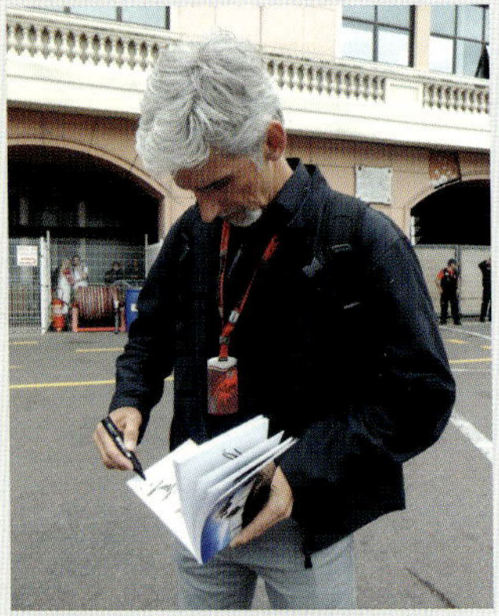

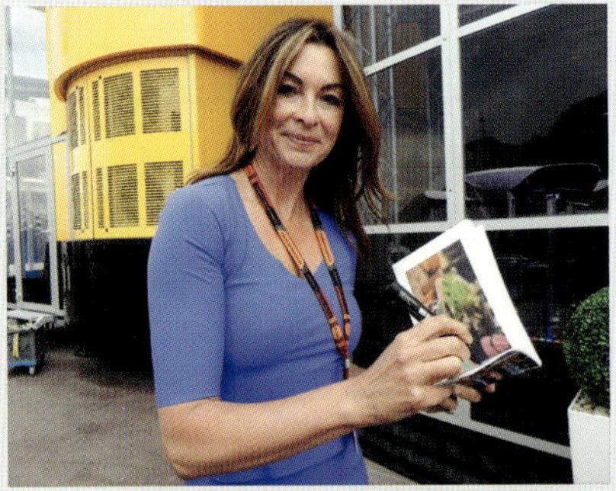

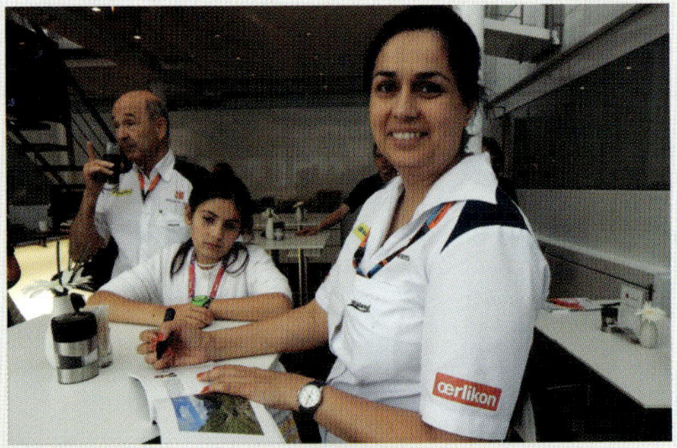

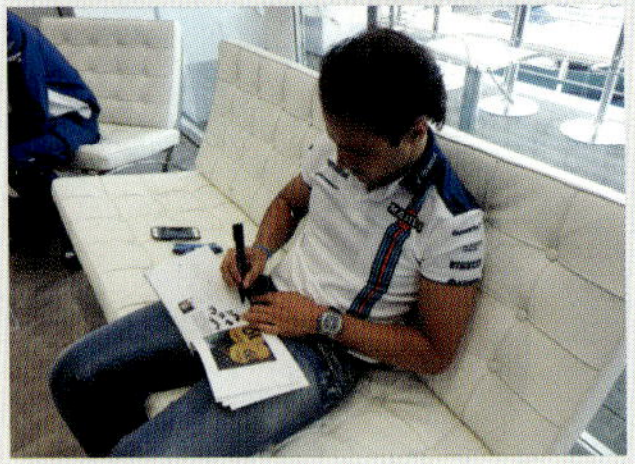

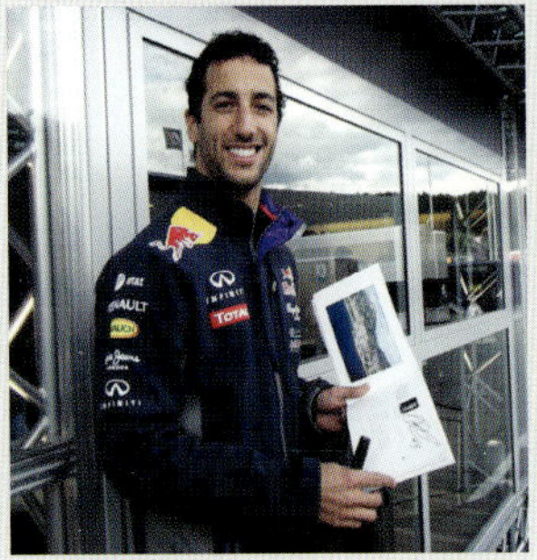

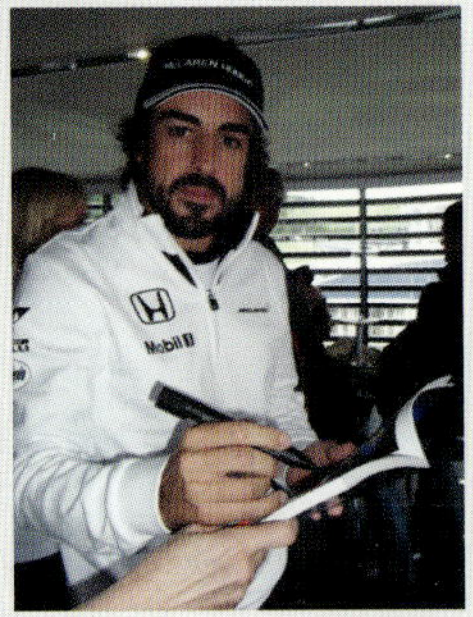

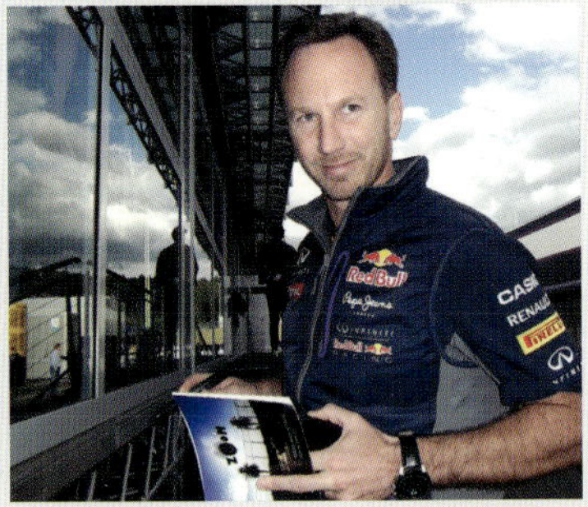